MAY–AUGUST 2014

mettle

BIBLE READING NOTES

TO INSPIRE COURAGE SPIRIT CHARACTER

yfc CWR

FSC www.fsc.org
MIX
Paper from responsible sources
FSC® C013417

Published 2014 by CWR, Waverley Abbey House, Waverley Lane, Farnham, Surrey GU9 8EP, England. Registered Charity No. 294387. Registered Limited Company No. 1990308.

Mettle Bible-reading notes are produced in association with British Youth for Christ. British Youth for Christ is part of Youth for Christ International, a movement of youth evangelism organisations in over 100 countries of the world. Please visit www.yfci.org for the country nearest you.

Series Editor: Simeon Whiting

Contributors: Ruth Hassall, Chris Kidd, Hannah Kidd, Simeon Whiting

The notes on 'Creation' were previously published in *Mettle* May–Aug 2010.

See back of book for list of National Distributors.

Concept development by YFC and CWR.
Editing, design and production by CWR.

Printed in Croatia by Zrinski.

CONTENTS

CREATION PART 1	4
DATING PART 1	21
MONEY PART 1	35
APOLOGETICS 2, PART 1	49
CREATION PART 2	63
DATING PART 2	77
MONEY PART 2	91
APOLOGETICS 2, PART 2	105
CREATION PART 3	119

WELCOME TO mettle

COURAGE SPIRIT CHARACTER ...

THE WORLD WE live in is incredible. When you take a step back and look at it, you can't help but be amazed by the beauty, complexity and diversity in it. But when you've seen the beauty in the world, how do you come to terms with the disease and decay in it? Our Core readings will explore what it means for us to live in a creation which is beautiful but fallen, and how we should relate to the One who created it.

Moving on, we'll think about Dating: how we can form godly and healthy dating relationships, and where sex comes into it. We'll investigate Money, too, which can be a tricky subject. Everyone seems to be keen to have money, but how do we stay in control of it, rather than it controlling us? And finally, we'll continue where we left off last time, with the second part of our Apologetics series. (But don't worry if you missed the Jan–Apr edition. There's still plenty in here for you!)

SO READ ON, THINK, PRAY, DISCUSS AND BE BLESSED!

The *Mettle* Team

THURS 1 MAY

READ:
GENESIS 1:1–13

PT1

KEY VERSE
V1

'In the beginning God created ...'

CREATION

THEY SAY YOU should begin at the beginning. So what better place to begin our series on 'Creation', than right at the beginning of everything? The very first time the Bible mentions God, what is He doing? He's creating – making stuff. He's not judging people, getting angry or giving long lists of commandments. He's doing something incredible: making something out of nothing. The first thing the Bible tells us about God is that He's a creator. He brings order out of chaos; He brings shape and

1 2 3 4 5 6 7
7

colour out of darkness and emptiness; He brings life out of nothing.

If we look at the world around us, we can see how amazingly detailed and beautiful and vibrant it is. A flea can jump 150 times its own length and pull 160,000 times its own weight. The human eye can see up to 10 million different colours and I've read that 5 trillion hydrogen atoms can fit onto a pinhead. It's absolutely mind-boggling. It just doesn't make sense to believe that a world like this simply 'happened'. The world is such an amazing place because God made it! The world is wonderful because God is wonderful. It's in His nature to be creative, innovative and surprising, and He hasn't changed – He's still all of these things today.

Over the next few days, we'll be learning more about the wonderful world around us and what it can tell us about the God who made it. We'll also be thinking about our responsibilities to look after God's world. But, for now, just think about this ...

THINK

The same God who created the world and made it amazing is with you right now. What's more, He's interested in what's going on in your life. What do you want to say to Him?

7

1
2
3
4
5
6
7

READ:
GENESIS 1:14–19

KEY VERSE
v16

'He also made the stars.'

IN THE MIDDLE of God creating light, sky, land and sea, the sun and moon, trees and plants, there's a sentence in Genesis 1 – almost a throwaway comment – that you could easily overlook. 'He also made the stars' (v16). It makes it sound as if this was an easy, almost insignificant thing for God to do!

Space is huge. I mean, really huge. The nearest star to us (apart from our own sun) is Proxima Centauri. And Proxima Centauri is 4.2421 light years away. So if you travelled at the speed of light, it would still take you more than four years to get there! Or, to put it another way, imagine a '4' with thirteen '0's after it, and that's approximately the number of kilometres between us and our nearest star other than the sun. Our own galaxy is just one of millions of galaxies in the universe. The numbers and the distances involved are just mind-boggling. Space is absolutely vast. And our God created it!

CHALLENGE

See what you can find out about the universe. Visit a few websites, and learn about some different stars and constellations. Find out what a black hole is or what happens when a star dies. Why not borrow a telescope and see what you can see on a clear night?

WEEKEND
3/4 MAY

READ:
GENESIS 1:20–25

KEY VERSE
v24

'Let the earth produce every sort of animal ...'

SCIENTISTS HAVE DISCOVERED approximately 950,000 species of insects. Just think about that for a moment. That's 950,000 kinds of insect, all of which are slightly different. If that wasn't staggering enough, it's reckoned that there are still nearly nine million more species to discover. And I remind you, this is just the insects! To think that God went to the trouble of creating ten million different species of insects is just mind-blowing. Frankly, I'm amazed that He bothered.

There's immense diversity amongst the animals God created, too. So many animals are

CONTINUED⏩

CONTINUED

incredible, for all sorts of reasons. For a start, there are all those brightly coloured birds and fish. Then there are lions, which are impressive because they're so powerful. Hummingbirds have the 'wow' factor because of their ability to hover by beating their wings up to 90 times a second! Giraffes are amazing too, if you think about it. They might look funny, but they were designed that way so that they could reach to eat leaves from tall trees.

When you think about it, the really impressive thing is how diverse all the animals in the world are. There's a massive range of shapes, sizes, textures, colours and abilities. And what does that tell us? If God created animals with that kind of diversity, He must be stunningly creative and have an incredible eye for detail. Not to mention His ability to work in surprising ways. Who else but God would have thought to give the chameleon the ability to change colour?

CHALLENGE

Go to the zoo! Or watch a wildlife documentary. (The BBC Planet Earth series is brilliant.) See how diverse and wonderfully designed the animal kingdom is. Then praise God for being such an amazing Creator.

READ:
GENESIS 1:26–30

KEY VERSE
v28

'Fill the earth and govern it.'

YOUR PARENTS ARE out of town for the weekend. 'Brilliant!' you think, 'I'm in charge!' So what might happen? You eat what you want from the fridge. You play your music at full volume. You push your little brother around. You invite all your friends round. You have a great time. When your parents get home, they find the fridge empty, your little brother in tears and the neighbours angry about all the noise.

God has put us in charge of the world He created. Some people misunderstand this and think that the world is ours, that we can do what we like with it and that the consequences don't matter. It's this kind of thinking that leads to pollution, climate change and the extinction of more and more species of animals.

This really isn't what God had in mind. He put us in charge of creation to look after it. It's ours to look after, but we don't own it – it's still God's. God created a beautiful world – and He's given us the responsibility to keep it that way.

PRAY

Lord, I'm sorry for the times when I take the world for granted. Help me to remember that I have a responsibility to look after creation. Help me to see what I can do to keep the world beautiful. Amen.

TUES 6 MAY

READ:
GENESIS 1:31–2:3

KEY VERSE
v1:31

'Then God looked over all he had made, and he saw that it was very good!'

LAST YEAR, A friend and I went to climb Snowdon, the highest mountain in Wales. Even though the weather was terrible, it was still a lot of fun and a brilliant day. There was one particular moment that literally almost took my breath away. The path took us over a ridge and suddenly, right in front of us, was a stunning view. Beneath us was a perfectly still mountain lake. Above it was the summit of the mountain, reaching into the clouds. And at that exact moment, the clouds parted and the sun streamed through and lit up the whole scene. It completely took me by surprise, but it reminded me instantly of how good the world is, and how good God is.

It's funny how easy it is to take the world for granted. But, every so often, as I found on Snowdon, we're reminded of just how good the world is. Really, it's impossible to ignore. The world God created is amazing. When we see that, all we can do is praise God for what He's made.

THINK

Whatever you're doing today, ask God to show you how good the world is. Then look around you. What do you see?

READ: COLOSSIANS 1:15–17

KEY VERSE v17

'He existed before anything else, and he holds all creation together.'

HAVE YOU EVER tried making bread without flour? Or mixing cement without sand? I once tried to make my mum a jewellery box. I was sure I knew what I was doing. Unfortunately, I chose to make it out of paper, without anything to reinforce it. Bread without flour would be a useless mess. A wall made without sand in the cement would fall down in no time. And I'm afraid my paper jewellery box just collapsed. (Mum was still very nice about it though.) If you miss out a crucial part of something, you shouldn't be surprised when that thing falls apart.

You might not even notice that crucial part when it's there, but as soon as it's gone, things start to go badly wrong. When God created the world, He created it perfectly and set the laws of nature in place – day and night, the rising and setting sun, wind and rain. Even though, as a result of the Fall, sin has caused the perfection to be flawed in some ways, it is still Christ who holds all things together. And it's Jesus who looks after us too. A lot of the time, we might not even be aware of what Jesus is doing, but we can be sure that if He wasn't there, everything around us would fall apart!

PRAY

Jesus, You are the single most important person in all creation. Thank You for holding all things together, even when I can't see You doing that. Amen.

THURS 8 MAY

READ:
ROMANS 4:16–22

KEY VERSE
v17

'... the God who gives life to the dead and calls into being things that were not.' (NIV)

NOTHING IS IMPOSSIBLE for God. Just ask Abraham! Put yourself in Abraham's place for a minute. God has promised you so many descendants that you won't be able to count them. But you're nearly 100, your wife isn't getting any younger either, and so far you haven't managed to produce a single baby! In these circumstances, you'd be forgiven for wondering whether maybe God had forgotten about you. Did Abraham begin to think like that? We don't know for sure. But we do know that, deep down, he never stopped believing that God would keep His promise. And that's exactly what happened.

Abraham knew that God was faithful, and he also knew that God could still work in seemingly impossible situations. The same is true today. Our God is Abraham's God: 'the God who gives life to the dead and calls things that are not as though they were'. God can create something incredible out of nothing. God gave a couple of pensioners a baby, and He can create awesome things in our lives too.

THINK

Is there any area of your life where you've stopped believing that God can turn things around? Spend a while remembering the times in the past when God has kept His promises and done brilliant stuff for you. Talk this over with a friend if it helps.

READ:
ROMANS 1:18–23

KEY VERSE
v20

'Through everything God made, [people] can clearly see his invisible qualities – his eternal power and divine nature.'

I RECENTLY ACQUIRED a brilliant new phone. For a start it looks really cool and is easy to use. Then, I can also download all my favourite music onto it, plus games and applications. The only problem is: it's difficult to leave my phone alone and do some work! But, however clever my phone is, it's not the phone itself that's really impressive – it's the people who designed it.

Today's verses remind us that something similar is true about the world. It's an amazing place. We've already mentioned how intricate, detailed and beautiful it is. But we're missing the point if we admire the world itself and forget the God who put it together.

Everything in creation points us towards God. It's as though His fingerprints are all over it. Some people refuse to see that (which is sad, because they're missing out on so much), and they should be careful – ignoring God is a dangerous thing to do. Others, perhaps, can see God's fingerprints in creation, but don't know who God is because nobody's told them. We're the ones who should be telling them!

CHALLENGE

Are you ignoring God? Perhaps you admire the world itself. Maybe you even call yourself a Christian, go to church and read the Bible and these *Mettle* notes. But when it really matters, you choose to ignore God and go your own way. If so, you're missing out! Choose today to worship God our Creator.

WEEKEND
10/11 MAY

READ:
ISAIAH 40:12–15

KEY VERSE
v13

'Who is able to advise the Spirit of the LORD? Who knows enough to give him advice or teach him?'

SOMETIMES IN LIFE things don't happen in the way we want or expect them to. A few years ago, I met a girl I thought was great. I really fancied her and, for a while, it looked as though we were going to get together. But just when things seemed to be going really well between us, she told me that she was moving away and didn't want to start going out with me because she didn't want a long-distance relationship. Ouch. At times like these, it can be easy to grumble at God and sulk because

He hasn't worked things out our way. And that's exactly what I did! Actually, when we do that, what we're saying to God is that we think we know better than He does.

Isaiah shows us that thinking like this is just daft. He does this by reminding us who God is and what He has done. Our God put the mountains together. His hands are big enough to hold the oceans. To God, the whole world, which might seem huge to us, is as tiny as a grain of sand! If God is this big and this powerful, what makes us think that we could know better than Him?! Our God is incredibly creative and awesomely powerful, and He's also infinitely wise. Even if we don't understand what God is doing in a particular situation, His way is always the best.

And that girl I mentioned? I never saw her again. But if I'd gone out with her, I'd probably never have met the girl I'm now married to – and my son would never have happened! Looks like God knew what He was doing after all!

PRAY

Are you or someone you know going through a difficult situation? Spend some time praying about it. Then trust God to deal with the situation in the way that's truly the best.

READ:
ROMANS 8:18–25

KEY VERSES
vv20–21

'But ... the creation looks forward to the day when it will join God's children in glorious freedom from death and decay.'

YOU'VE PROBABLY NOTICED that, although the world is an amazing place, there are times when things go wrong with it. We've all seen photos of the scenes after earthquakes, freak storms or volcanic eruptions. The horrific aftermath of the Philippine typhoon is still fresh in our minds too, even though it happened last year. So if creation is good, and the God who created it is good, why do awful things like these happen? That's a difficult question to answer, but these verses from Romans give us a few clues.

The world is flawed – under a curse (v20) – not because God planned it this way, but as a result of the Fall (see Gen. 3:17–19). The devil loves to destroy anything good, and we can see his influence in the world. We're all flawed too (v23). All too often, it's our choices that damage ourselves, the people around us, and creation as well. (We'll look at this a bit more tomorrow.) However, in Romans 8, the apostle Paul tells us something really important: whatever the reasons for the flaws in creation, one day God will make it perfect! He'll make us and the whole of creation new and flawless – and pain and suffering will end.

PRAY

Lord God, please break the devil's influence on the world. May Your plans work, not his. Thank You that, one day, You'll make everything new and flawless and exactly as You want it. Amen.

READ: GENESIS 3:1–19

KEY VERSE
v17

'... the ground is cursed because of you.'

I DON'T ENJOY doing laundry. And on one occasion doing my laundry was even less fun than usual. I used to load my clothes into a spin dryer, once they'd finished in the washing machine. I'd put the end of the hose from the back of the dryer into the sink, and switch it on. On this particular day, I switched on the spin dryer then left the room to do something else. When I came back, the hose had come out of the sink and was snaking around the floor – and water was gushing all over the kitchen! Cleaning up the mess was not fun.

That day, I learned that my actions affect my environment. My careless attitude led to a whole lot of mess. God's plan is for us to take care of His creation, but how often do we not think about it? Small careless actions like littering or not thinking about our carbon footprint can pollute the world and leave it in a real mess.

Our reading in Genesis goes further than this too. In a way, every time we disobey God it has an impact on the world around us. When we go against God's plan, it damages us, it pollutes our relationships with other people, and it even pollutes God's creation.

THINK

Do any of your actions, however small, pollute the world around you? Do you disobey God by any of your actions? Say sorry to God for these things, and think of some ways in which you can help to clear up the mess in our world.

READ:
JOHN 3:16–21

KEY VERSE
v17

'God sent his Son into the world not to judge the world, but to save the world through him.'

A WHILE AGO, I went to see my doctor. My heartbeat was doing funny things; it felt very strange and a little bit worrying. How do you think the doctor responded? Did he shout and yell at me because I was sick? Did he tell me what a terrible person I was for getting into that state? Of course not! That's not what doctors do! He took a good look at me, worked out what the problem was and told me what I needed to do to get better. (Turns out, if I just drank a bit less coffee my heart would sort itself out.)

Our world is 'sick'. People act and speak in ways that are selfish, irresponsible and hurtful. We see it all around us and, if we're honest, we know that we've acted like that ourselves. This behaviour leaves the world in a mess. But God had a plan. He sent Jesus into the world, not to shout and yell at everybody and tell us how terrible we were, but to show us the way to be healed.

Our sins and mistakes impact both us and our world, leaving it in a real mess. However, Jesus came to save us, forgive us and sort out the mess. God has a plan to save our world.

PRAY

Lord Jesus, thank You for coming to forgive our sins and save the world. Thank You that I can be forgiven too. Please forgive me for all the times I've said and done things which were selfish and which made the world more of a mess. Amen.

READ: EPHESIANS 2:1–10

KEY VERSE v8

'For it is by grace you have been saved, through faith ... it is the gift of God ...' (NIV)

WE MENTIONED YESTERDAY that Jesus came into the world to save us and deal with our sin. This was God's plan to deal with the mess we'd made. Today, we find out that His plan is for everyone to be free from sin and to discover the amazing life He offers. It's a free gift! We can't do anything to deserve it, and all we need to do to receive it is to ask. But God doesn't force His plan on us – it's up to us individually to choose this.

Yesterday, I told you about a time when I was sick and went to the doctor. The doctor helped me, and after that I was fine. But what if I'd decided I'd be OK and chosen not to go to the doctor? If I'd been ill with something serious, it would have got worse and worse until it killed me. Sin is like that. If we don't do anything about it, we stay sick on the inside and separated from God; sin eventually destroys us. If we choose to turn to Jesus, He'll deal with our sin and give us life – but it's our choice whether or not to turn to Him. A lot of people seem to choose to ignore Jesus. They just don't realise how much they need His help.

God's plan is for everyone to be saved, but each person has to choose whether or not they want to go along with His plan.

CHALLENGE

Do your friends and family know about God's plan? Could you be the person to tell them?

READ:
PSALM 8:1–9

KEY VERSE
v1

'O LORD, our Lord, your majestic name fills the earth!'

OVER THE PAST couple of weeks we've talked about how incredible God's creation is. We've mentioned space and just how vast it is. We've touched on the staggering detail and intricacy of the world and the jaw-dropping diversity in the animal kingdom. We've also looked at our own responsibility to act in a way that looks after creation, rather than damages it.

But above all, creation points us towards God. The universe tells us that God is immensely powerful, creative and surprising. It shows us that He has an incredible eye for detail. (It also shows us how much He loves us – and we'll talk about that more next month.) God is the One who created the world, cares for it and holds it together. What's more, He still creates now, by bringing life and hope into impossible situations. When we look at creation, our response should be the same as the writer of this psalm. Quite simply, we should worship God for being so wonderful, powerful and creative.

PRAY

Take some time to worship God now. Thank Him for the beauty of creation and praise Him for being amazing. Why not sit in your garden or go for a walk in the park to get inspiration?

READ:
GENESIS 2:18–24

KEY VERSE
V18

'Then the LORD God said, "It is not good for the man to be alone. I will make a helper who is just right for him."'

PT1 DATING

DESIGNED TO BE IN RELATIONSHIP

DATING: WHAT CONNOTATIONS does this word have for you? Are they positive or negative? Perhaps you're in a long-term committed relationship. Perhaps you enjoy playing the field. Or maybe you just wish you could find your soul mate. Do you think God has anything to say about dating? Over the next couple of weeks we will begin to find out what the Bible has to tell us about this important area of life.

Dating is a relatively modern phenomenon, so there are not many explicit references to dating, as we would

CONTINUED»

CONTINUED

understand it, in the Bible. However, the Bible has a lot to say about relationships in general, and this can shed important light on what God might say to us about our dating habits today.

First and foremost, God created us to be people in relationship with others. In today's key verse, we read about the first time God found something in His creation that wasn't good: 'It is not good for the man to be alone' (Gen. 2:18). God saw that Adam could be and do much more with a companion.

God's intention was that Eve would be a 'helper' for Adam, someone who would support him and encourage him in every area of life. In view of this, let's look at our closest relationships. Do the people closest to us support us in every area of our lives? In particular, do they help us to live the life that God intends for us and do the work that He is calling us to do?

THINK

Whether you are currently dating or not, think about your closest relationships. Do your close friends support you in living your life for Christ or do they hinder this?

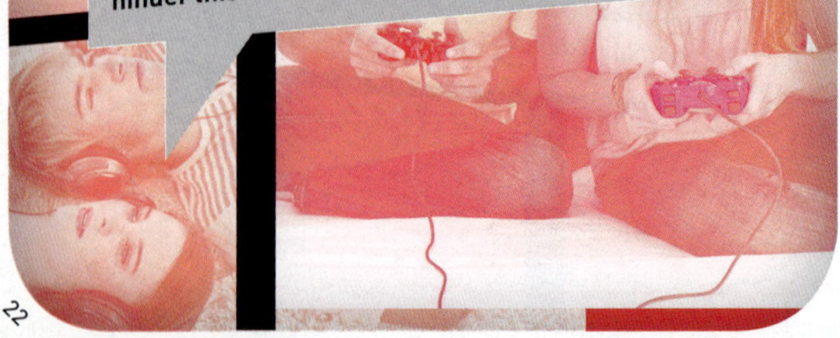

READ: ECCLESIASTES 4:9–12

KEY VERSE v12

'Three are even better, for a triple-braided cord is not easily broken.'

TODAY'S READING REINFORCES that God's intention for us is to be in relationships with others. This does not necessarily mean romantic relationships, but there are many advantages to supporting and being supported by others. Look through today's passage – what advantages are listed to being in a pair? What other advantages could you add to these from your own experience?

Just like we saw yesterday, God sees our need for companionship. However, rather than just stopping at saying that two are better than one, this passage says that 'Three are even better' (Eccl. 4:12).

This passage reminds us of a very important truth. No matter how good our earthly relationships might be, including God in them will strengthen and enhance them to their full potential. Yes, the third person is God.

The image of the cord is very powerful too. It suggests that God should not be an afterthought in our relationships. Rather, He should be entwined with us; deeply involved in our relationships and as much part of them as each of the people involved.

PRAY

Invite God to become part of your earthly relationships. Ask Him to strengthen them and make them healthy and sustaining.

READ:
GENESIS 3:11–13

KEY VERSE
v12

'The man replied, "It was the woman you gave me who gave me the fruit, and I ate it."'

WE HAVE ALREADY seen that God recognises mankind's need for relationships. We have seen how He provided Eve as a companion for Adam and that this relationship was part of His perfect plan for mankind. However, this relationship was not without its problems!

In today's reading, we rejoin the story of Adam and Eve after they have sinned by eating the fruit that God had forbidden them to eat. They both know that they have done wrong, and try to hide from God. When God confronts them, we then see them try to avoid the blame.

One of the common pitfalls within relationships is doing something you know is wrong and then trying to blame the other person. When we are close to other people, we all too often find it easy to blame them for our own mistakes and wrongdoing. It is no use hiding from God, though – He can see what's in our hearts. And reflecting back on yesterday's passage we need to be completely open with Him, remembering that He is the third person in our relationships.

CHALLENGE

How much do you take responsibility for your own actions and how often do you try to pass the blame onto others? Are there any bad habits within your relationships which you need to step up and change?

READ: PROVERBS 4:23–27

KEY VERSE v23

'Guard your heart above all else, for it determines the course of your life.'

SPEND A FEW minutes reflecting on that verse from Proverbs. How much do you think it's true for you that 'your heart ... determines the course of your life' (Prov. 4:23)? If you think that you love someone, does this change the way you see your life and the path set out for your future?

Perhaps you feel that a particular university course would be good for you but you are considering not going because you can't bear the thought of being away from your boyfriend/girlfriend. Perhaps you always thought you would want to take a gap year to serve God but now you're having second thoughts because of how it might affect your relationship.

A strong and healthy relationship is a wonderful thing, but it should not stop us from following where God leads us – and after all aren't we here to live out His will, not our own? Our priority should be to 'Seek the Kingdom of God above all else'. God knows us better than we know ourselves. If you can put your trust in Him and seek His will, you can be confident that He will 'give you everything you need' (Matt. 6:33).

THINK

Today's passage talks about us making a straight path for our feet (Prov. 4:26). How far do you let God guide you in your decisions and how much are you influenced by your relationships?

THURS 22 MAY

READ:
ACTS 20:18–27

KEY VERSE
v24

'But my life is worth nothing to me unless I use it for finishing the work assigned me by the Lord Jesus ...'

ALTHOUGH I'M EMBARRASSED to admit it, I'll let you in to a secret. As a child, every time I blew out my birthday candles, I used to wish for a boyfriend. To me, this was the ultimate thing to aim for and would make life meaningful and complete! Fairy tales fuelled my belief that being loved by somebody is the real sign of having value and worth.

Let me tell you now, there is no truth at all in the view that you have to be in a romantic relationship to have any kind of value. Paul tells us that his life and ours are made worthwhile by doing what God wants us to do and 'finishing the work assigned ... by the Lord Jesus' (Acts 20:24). This is something we can do whether we are single or in a relationship.

In one of his letters, Paul highlights that we may be better able to focus on doing God's work when we are not hindered by a relationship. But perhaps the most important verse for us to reflect on is this: 'I want you to do whatever will help you serve the Lord best, with as few distractions as possible' (1 Cor. 7:35).

CHALLENGE

God has a plan for you and for your life. Are you following the path that God has set for you? Are any of your relationships hindering you in that? Do you need to let a relationship go so that you can serve God more faithfully?

READ: 2 CORINTHIANS 6:14–16

KEY VERSES
vv14–15

'Don't team up with those who are unbelievers ... How can a believer be a partner with an unbeliever?'

WHEN I WAS at primary school I remember one particular sports day when I did the three-legged race. My friend and I were a disaster zone! We barely made it to the finish line, despite our determination to help each other and head in the same direction. Imagine the mess we would have been in if we'd had different ideas about the way to go.

Whether or not we should date non-Christians is a contentious issue. But these verses from 2 Corinthians highlight a problem with that kind of relationship. Whatever our relationship status, our ultimate focus should be in living out God's will for our lives. How can we do that if the person we're dating doesn't share that priority?

It's not that dating a non-Christian is 'wrong', but it isn't what's best. How can we form a lasting, supportive relationship with someone we differ from on such a basic level? Where something as important as faith isn't shared between the two people, it's not fair for either person.

PRAY

Thank God for couples you know who have supported each other in their walk with God. Also pray for couples you know who are not both Christians. Ask God to help Christians in relationships with non-Christians to keep their focus on Him.

WEEKEND
24/25 MAY

READ:
PSALM 37:23–26

KEY VERSE
v23

'The LORD directs the steps of the godly. He delights in every detail of their lives.'

HAVE YOU EVER spent ages on hold to a call centre somewhere? You ring them with an important question but end up waiting to talk to someone for what feels like forever, being told repeatedly by a recorded message that, 'Your call is important to us'. Whenever this happens to me, I can't help suspecting that my call really can't be that important to them if they won't answer it!

When we talk to God, He is always there to listen to us. He has a limitless ability to hear everyone, all over the world, all the time. I love the passage in the New Testament where we read that God even knows each individual sparrow (Luke 12:6).

Of course, God is concerned with the big, important, global issues. But, today's reading tells us that God 'delights in every detail' of our lives. This includes our love life! He cares about how we are feeling, who we are falling for, and what worries us. He wants to be included in these details and wants us to share our hopes and fears with Him. Don't ever think that God isn't interested or can't be bothered with you.

Over the next week we will be looking at the love lives of a few people in the Bible. In the same way as God cares about us, these people's relationships were important to God. As we read their stories, reflect on how you think their relationships affected their ability to serve God and live out their God-given purposes.

CHALLENGE

Spend some time talking with God now about your private thoughts and what's really on your mind and heart. Remember that God 'delights in every detail' of your life. You can trust Him with anything.

MON 26 MAY

READ:
GENESIS 29:14B–30

KEY VERSE
v20

'So Jacob worked seven years to pay for Rachel ... his love for her was so strong that it seemed to him but a few days.'

HAVE YOU EVER tried to do anything to prove your love for someone? Perhaps you've bought an extravagant gift, or agreed to do some kind of horrible task for them. In today's reading, we see how Jacob has fallen for Rachel and agreed to work for her father for seven years. (Yes, really! That's the equivalent of school years 7–13!)

At the end of these seven years of labour, Jacob is tricked. Rather than being given Rachel as his wife, he is given her older sister, Leah. After Jacob's protests, he is given Rachel as his wife as well but has to work an additional seven years for this! Now we're looking at the equivalent of years 7-13, three years of university and four years of work after that! Would you be prepared to work that long for anyone, no matter how much you loved them? What about just waiting that long? Perhaps you are waiting for that person now, either waiting to meet the right person or to be in a relationship with someone in particular.

God set us a great example of going to extreme lengths to show His love – He sent His only Son to die so that we could know Him. He was that desperate for a relationship with us.

THINK
When we are waiting for the one we love (or will love), how can we have the right patient attitude and how can we show our love and commitment?

READ: GENESIS 29:31–35

KEY VERSE v31

'When the LORD saw that Leah was unloved, he enabled her to have children, but Rachel could not conceive.'

WHEN WE LOOKED at yesterday's passage from Genesis, who did you identify with in the story? Perhaps it wasn't so much Jacob, working for fourteen years to win the girl he loved. Perhaps you feel that you're more like Leah, the misfit; the one who always seems to get left behind when everyone else is dating. Even if you don't identify with Leah, I am sure you can think of someone you know who fits that description.

Thankfully, the story isn't all bad for Leah. In today's reading we read on from yesterday and we see that God saw Leah's suffering and blessed her by enabling her to conceive several children.

If you feel insignificant in the eyes of your peers, then take heart from this story. God sees your pain and He loves you dearly. We mentioned at the weekend that God is concerned with every detail of our lives. Leah's story is a real illustration of this!

By the way, notice that Leah is always trying to find love and acceptance from her husband. But when she has her last son she says, 'Now I will praise the LORD' (Gen. 29:35), finally acknowledging the true source of love and acceptance!

PRAY

Father God, we all feel unlovable sometimes. Help me to remember the love that You have for me and find comfort in that. Amen.

READ:
JUDGES 16:4–21

KEY VERSE
v15

'..."How can you tell me, 'I love you,' when you don't share your secrets with me?"'

HAVE YOU EVER heard the phrase 'love is blind'? Perhaps the story of Samson and Delilah illustrates that idea. Samson falls in love with Delilah, but seems oblivious to the fact that Delilah clearly doesn't feel the same way. Delilah sees her relationship with Samson as an opportunity to make money. All she needs to do is get Samson to tell her the secret of his strength.

After Delilah's constant nagging and emotional blackmail, Samson gives in and tells her everything. Given the fact that every time he has told her a lie she has acted on it to try and bring about his downfall, Samson does seem more than a little foolish to have actually told her the truth. But, as we have said, love is blind. Sometimes our love for someone can make us do things we later regret.

We can be persuaded to do many unwise things by someone we think we love. This might mean going further in our physical relationship than we want to, spending all our money on extravagant gifts, or making unwise decisions about our future to impress them. When we want to please someone we care about, it can be very difficult to say no.

THINK

Can you think of any situations where you are under pressure to do something you don't think is right? What can we learn from the story of Samson and Delilah?

READ: MATTHEW 1:18–25

KEY VERSE v24

'When Joseph woke up, he did as the angel of the Lord commanded and took Mary as his wife.'

JOSEPH AND MARY are one of the most inspiring couples in the Bible. We're going to spend the next two days looking at their story and what we can learn from them.

Imagine what Joseph goes through. He is meant to be marrying Mary but then finds out she is pregnant. He knows that the baby is not his and therefore his only real option is to end their relationship. Imagine how you would feel if you were in his situation. I'm not sure I would find it easy to be as honourable and dignified as Joseph and just decide to end the relationship on the quiet. But then, when an angel appears to Joseph and tells him to take Mary as his wife, Joseph obeys God's command, however hard it must have seemed.

Sometimes our relationships hit tricky patches and we're not sure whether we're doing the right thing in staying with that person. But as we've already said, God cares about all the details of our lives and He wants to guide us. Are we open to His guidance on whether or not we should stay in a relationship with somebody?

PRAY

Father God, thank You for Joseph's example in following Your guidance even when it was hard. Please help me be as ready as Joseph to obey You in relationships, even when this doesn't seem like the logical thing to do. Amen.

FRI 30 MAY

READ:
MATTHEW 2:13–23

KEY VERSE
v13

'Flee to Egypt ... Stay there until I tell you to return, because Herod is going to search for the child to kill him.'

YESTERDAY WE TOOK a look at Joseph's willingness to obey God in his relationship with Mary. And the difficult times were far from over when Jesus was born. When Herod shows just how far he is prepared to go to make sure there's no other king to threaten him, Joseph and Mary have to take the young Jesus and flee to Egypt to avoid a massacre. Finally, quite some time later, God commands them to go back to Israel.

Throughout what we read about Joseph and Mary in the Bible, we see that they are always obedient to God's commands. They stick together, even when life is scary, confusing and uncertain, and support each other in trying to live as God wants them to. What a great example for us as we seek to form our own God-honouring relationships.

Life isn't always rosy, but God calls us to support and encourage each other in the hard times, whether in romantic relationships or as friends and families. We have already looked at the fact that God recognises our need for relationship. He doesn't want us to be alone but wants us to have people who can support us in living out God's will for us – just as Joseph and Mary supported each other.

CHALLENGE

When life gets hard, how does it affect your relationships? Are you committed to the people closest to you? Or do you lash out and shut yourself off from them?

READ:
MATTHEW 6:19-34

KEY VERSE
V21

'Wherever your treasure is, there the desires of your heart will also be.'

MONEY PT1

OVER THE NEXT couple of weeks we're going to be thinking about money, and what our attitude as Christians should be towards it. Money is something that can occupy a lot of a person's thinking space – if they feel they don't have enough, they worry about getting more and if they feel they have a lot, they worry about keeping it safe.

Interestingly, Jesus talks quite a lot about money and he tells a number of stories that involve it, particularly as recorded in Luke's gospel in chapters 18-22. Jesus never says that we should keep away from money –

CONTINUED▸▸

CONTINUED

He recognises that it's part of our daily life and a key means of survival – but He does warn us about the hold that money can have over us, if we treat it as more important than it really is. Jesus tells stories of what happens when money becomes our security, or when it becomes a way in which we measure our status.

In today's reading, Jesus warns about what happens when money becomes our focus. If it becomes our 'treasure' then that's what we will value and concentrate on, rather than trusting God. He makes it very clear that we cannot focus on both God and money – when we look at one, we will turn our backs on the other. We shouldn't get caught up in the money obsession that the world has, because God will provide us with all that we need. If we believe that to be true, then we will be able to be generous with what we have, whether that's a lot or just a little.

THINK

As you read through this passage, which of the things that Jesus mentions do you find yourself worrying most about? Clothes? Food? Where you live? How do you respond to what Jesus says about worrying about those things?

READ: LUKE 12:13-34

KEY VERSE v15

'Beware! Guard against every kind of greed. Life is not measured by how much you own.'

WHEN I WATCH the adverts on television I wonder if anyone in the advertising industry ever read any of Jesus' words. It would appear not. So often these days, we're given the message that you are what you own, so it had better be the best and the latest if you want people to think well of you. The advertising business depends on us always being dissatisfied with what we currently have, and always wanting more and better.

Jesus' response to someone who wanted more was to tell a story. He told a parable about a man who lived his life in pursuit of more, who thought that his worth was measured by the volume of what he owned and that the security of his future depended upon it. Sadly, the man in the story found out the hard way that he had put his security in the wrong things. All his gains turned out to be for nothing.

It's very easy for us to fall into this trap too. So, we need to guard ourselves against this way of thinking and find our worth and security in our relationship with God and all with which He has blessed us.

CHALLENGE

The next time you see an advert and you're tempted to buy the product in question, ask yourself what your real reason is for wanting it. Is it really something you need?

TUES 3 JUN

READ:
LUKE 18:18-30

KEY VERSE
v22

'Sell all your possessions and give the money to the poor, and you will have treasure in heaven. Then come, follow me.'

THIS HAS GOT to be one of the saddest stories recorded in the gospel. It's the story of a rich young man who desperately wanted to be right with God, but wasn't willing to make God the priority in his life. In many other aspects of his life he had been able to act in the right way, but when it came to parting with his money, he just couldn't do it. Jesus knew that while these things were so important to him, the man wouldn't truly be able to follow Him.

Jesus isn't saying that it's wrong to be rich. But He is saying that it is damaging when money has such a strong hold on you that you can't bear to give it away. The rich young man thought that what he wanted more than anything was eternal life, but Jesus exposed what was really going on in his heart – the man did want treasure in heaven, but he also wanted to hold on to his treasure on earth.

Jesus' promise to everyone listening was that if you are willing to give up what you have for His sake, you won't regret it: you will have what you need in this life and gain the eternal life that the young man so desperately wanted.

PRAY

God, please would You help me to look honestly at my heart to see if there is anything there more important than You. Please help me to put You first.

READ:
LUKE 19:1-10

KEY VERSE
v9

'Salvation has come to this home today, for this man has shown himself to be a true son of Abraham.'

IN THE PASSAGE we looked at yesterday from Luke 18, Jesus says that it's hard for the rich to enter the kingdom of God, but that all things are possible with God – even changing a person's heart. Here, we have the evidence of that. It's the story of a rich man – and not just rich, but deceitful too – whose heart was changed completely when he met Jesus.

Tax collectors were notorious in Israel for not just collecting taxes that were owed but for collecting more than was necessary and keeping it for themselves. Zacchaeus was a chief tax collector and had become very wealthy from his ill-gotten gains. The bystanders were very disgruntled that Jesus would have tea with a man like this, but Jesus knew exactly what Zacchaeus was like and the place that money had in his life. Zacchaeus knew that he couldn't be a friend of Jesus and continue with his life as it was, so he immediately committed to paying back much more than he'd taken and giving half of his wealth to the poor. In doing these things, he proved that money was no longer his priority; Jesus was.

THINK

Jesus said that Zacchaeus became a son of Abraham; someone who, like Abraham, believed in God and proved that by what he did. Does the way you handle money demonstrate what you believe?

READ:
LUKE 21:1-4

KEY VERSE
v4

'For they have given a tiny part of their surplus, but she, poor as she is, has given everything she has.'

FOR THE DISCIPLES, life with Jesus must have meant being constantly challenged on what they thought they knew. You can just imagine them standing with Jesus and watching the crowds making their offerings in the Temple, being really impressed with the amounts of money that some people put in the collection box. In the eyes of the disciples, these people were incredibly generous. But this turns out to be another of those challenging moments for the disciples as Jesus gives them a powerful lesson on giving. He would have known that the disciples respected those who gave the most, but the person who caught Jesus' attention was the poor widow who gave just a couple of pennies.

For Jesus, generosity is not defined by how much you give; it's about how much of a sacrifice it is for you to give. Jesus wanted the disciples to know that although they might be impressed by large offerings, those rich people would barely feel the impact of what they'd given. On the other hand, the widow would feel it deeply and immediately. She was the one who gave until it hurt and trusted God to provide for what she herself needed. She was the one who was truly generous.

PRAY

Thank You, Jesus, that You are not impressed by the amount of money that we give, but the heart with which we give it. Please help me to be truly generous. Amen.

READ: HEBREWS 13:1-6

KEY VERSE
v5

'... be satisfied with what you have. For God has said, "I will never fail you. I will never abandon you."'

I'M CURRENTLY READING a book by Jen Hatmaker called 7. It is a record of a project that Jen undertook when she became shocked at her level of consumerism. Jen realised that she wasn't simply buying stuff (as we all do); she was buying stuff in ever-greater amounts and never really satisfied with what she had.

So, Jen decided to tackle her excesses in clothing, shopping, waste, food, possessions, media and stress. She set herself the challenge of living with just seven things in each of these areas. For one month, she only allowed herself to wear seven items of clothing (not including underwear!). Through it, she was appalled at how many clothes she owned but never wore. But what upset her more was how much she relied on her clothes to give her identity and how much she worried about what others would think of her. She was depending on these things to give her what only God could.

Consumerism always leaves us wanting more. It will never really satisfy us. God longs for us to be satisfied in Him alone, to look to Him for our identity and to know that we can depend on Him to be with us always.

CHALLENGE

How much of a consumer do you think you are? How much of what you own do you actually use? If you own stuff you never use, give it away.

WEEKEND

7/8 JUN

READ:
1 TIMOTHY 6:6-10

KEY VERSE
v10

'For the love of money is the root of all kinds of evil. And some people, craving money, have wandered from the true faith ...'

THIS HAS GOT to be one of the most often misquoted verses in the Bible! You may well have heard people quote that 'money is the root of all evil', but that's not what Paul says. It's the *love* of money that causes trouble, and in the situation that Paul is writing to Timothy about, it's causing people to neglect their faith and prioritise the pursuit of wealth. Money has become their god.

There is nothing wrong with money and possessions in themselves, which you may be relieved to hear as you look around your room at your possessions! The problems come, as we have seen over this last week, from the position they occupy in our lives and our attitude towards them. When they become our god, we are in real danger.

As you read about the first Christians in the New Testament, you see that they didn't make a priority of material riches: far from it. They very often gave money away and shared possessions. They strove to become rich in faith, rich in generosity and rich in good deeds. These are the riches that we should love. Paul tells Timothy to urge the people around him who are materially rich to aim for riches in other ways instead.

In Philippians (another letter written by Paul), he says that he has learned to be content whatever the circumstances. He has known times when he had plenty, and has known times when he had very little, yet in all those times he knew real contentment because he knew God. He'd enjoyed things when he had them but he didn't sink into despair when he didn't.

CHALLENGE

Make a point this week of giving away more money than you usually would. For example, start a regular monthly donation to a charity or give one large gift to your church for something specific.

READ:
1 TIMOTHY 6:17-21

KEY VERSE
v18

'They should be rich in good works and generous to those in need, always being ready to share with others.'

A LITTLE WHILE ago I spent some time in Cambodia and what struck me most was the level of poverty in which most people lived. For the first time in my life I met people who really had nothing other than the clothes they were wearing. The reality is that I have been privileged to be born in the western world, which means that though I may not be particularly rich compared to some people in the West, I am incredibly rich compared to my friends in Cambodia.

When I got home, I felt guilty for a while about the amount of stuff that surrounded me and I even considered giving it all away. But I came to realise that trying to live like my Cambodian friends wasn't the answer. Instead, I should let my experiences prompt me to be a good steward of all that I have. I have been blessed with a nice home and a good salary, but I know that they are gifts from God that I can use to be a blessing to other people. When we have the attitude that everything we have is a gift from God, it changes our heart and loosens our grip on our money and possessions. God has entrusted us with good things and wants us to be generous with them.

THINK
Do you see all that you have been given as a gift from God? How would it change the way in which you treat your possessions if you believed that? Are you a good steward?

READ: PHILIPPIANS 4:10-20

KEY VERSE v19

'And this same God who takes care of me will supply all your needs from his glorious riches, which have been given to us in Christ Jesus.'

RECENTLY I WAS having a conversation with a friend about whether or not it's wrong to buy nice things and cool clothes. She told me a little about how she was brought up. Her parents gave her three cups with different labels on them: one said, 'Spend', another, 'Save' and the other, 'Give'. Her parents had encouraged her that whenever she got some money, whether pocket money, birthday money or money earned, she should distribute it amongst the three cups. Over the years she has continued this practice (with bank accounts rather than cups!) and if there's something that she would really like, she waits until she has enough money in the spending account to be able to buy it. This means that she is able to get the nice things that she likes, but often not immediately, and not at the expense of being able to respond to other people's needs.

The Bible doesn't say that it's wrong to have nice things. In fact there are many stories of rich people who were followers of God. The key thing is that these things don't consume us, and that we are still able to be generous to others.

CHALLENGE

Why don't you get three cups or jars and label them in the same way my friend did? Start distributing your money in this way, to make sure you're able to give to others.

WED 11 JUN

READ:
DEUTERONOMY 14:22-29

KEY VERSE
v22

'You must set aside a tithe of your crops – one-tenth of all the crops you harvest each year.'

THE IDEA OF giving is not a new one for Christians; God has instilled it in His people from long ago. In this reading we see God instructing the Israelites to give ten per cent of what they harvest back to Him. This has continued to be a rule of thumb amongst Christians. If you hear people talking about tithing, this is what it means.

The reality is, though, that this was just the beginning! On top of the tithe, the people were instructed to leave some crops in their fields for the poor to harvest and to give money to the priests, and to give further gifts for festivals and sacrifices. They really ended up giving more like 25 per cent of their income!

In the New Testament, the theme of giving is still very present, but it talks in terms of people giving cheerfully and generously, rather than a specific amount. The key thing in both the Old and New Testaments is that giving is meant to be something to be celebrated. It's a joyful thing, because it recognises that God has given us good things and reminds us to thank Him for that. So the question isn't, 'How little can I get away with giving?' but, 'How generous and cheerful can I be in what I give?'

PRAY

Lord, sometimes it feels hard to think about giving away what I have, especially if I don't think I have very much. Please help me to know real joy in being generous. Amen.

READ: DEUTERONOMY 8:6-18

KEY VERSE v18

'Remember the LORD your God. He is the one who gives you power to be successful ...'

WITH ALL THIS talk of giving you may still be wondering why you should. After all, aren't your money and possessions yours to do what you like with? Especially if you earned the money to buy them in the first place.

This is precisely the situation that God was addressing with the Israelites. He had brought them through the wilderness into the land that He had promised, flowing with milk and honey – meaning it was a rich and fertile land. They would be able to eat well, enjoy good harvests and prosper because resources were readily available. God knew that very quickly they would become rich and comfortable, so He warns them not to become proud in their wealth and beautiful homes. He wants them to remember the story of where they came from; how it was He who brought them to this beautiful place and gave them skills to enable them to earn their living.

When we are tempted to think that we have done everything on our own, we too should remember that warning. We should stop and thank God for giving us the ability to thrive and the skills we use to earn our living.

THINK

How would you respond to someone who says they have no need to thank God or give money away, because they are 'self-made'?

FRI 13 JUN

READ:
PSALM 34:1-10

KEY VERSE:
v8

'Taste and see that the LORD is good. Oh, the joys of those who take refuge in him!'

IN 1836, GEORGE Muller and his wife opened their home to 30 orphans. Over the years this number grew so much that they had to build five homes to accommodate all the children. Despite the huge costs of building and running these homes, Muller never asked people for money to support this work. He told many stories of how they received donations of food just when they were needed to feed the children. One breakfast time, when there was no food in the house, Muller got the children to sit down at the breakfast table and give thanks for their food. Just as they finished praying, there was a knock on the door and the baker stood there with enough bread to feed everyone. And just a moment later, the milkman's cart broke down right in front of their house, so he asked if they would like the milk as he could no longer deliver it!

Time and time again God tells us not to worry about our situation. He knows what we need and has promised to provide for us if we trust in Him. He doesn't want us to become so preoccupied with money and possessions that we forget to trust Him. If we don't trust Him, we don't have the joy of seeing Him keep His promises to us.

PRAY

Thank You, Lord, that You are good. Please help me to trust You in all situations. I trust Your promise that I will never lack anything I need. Amen.

READ:
2 TIMOTHY 3:10–17

KEY VERSE
V16

'All Scripture is inspired by God and is useful to teach us what is true and to make us realize what is wrong in our lives.'

PT1
APOLOGETICS 2

WELCOME BACK TO the Apologetics series. If you were with us for the January–April *Mettle*, you'll have covered a whole load of important apologetics-related material already. But don't worry if you missed it – we've got some great stuff to come, with loads to think about, discuss and pray over.

We've already looked at why it's important to be able to explain what we believe and why. We've picked apart some of the common arguments atheists raise against the Christian faith and thought about how we can counter those arguments. That included the

CONTINUED▸▸

CONTINUED

accusations that God is a bully, doesn't make any difference in the world and doesn't exist anyway. In this issue of *Mettle*, we're picking up where we left off last time: unpacking more important truths about our God and our world. Keep in mind that Apologetics doesn't mean 'apologising' for what we believe, but explaining it and supporting our views. It's about building bridges with people who believe different things, not about getting defensive.

Let's kick off by asking a few questions about the Bible. How do we know the Bible is reliable? Is it really relevant to us? And what are we supposed to make of those weird bits in Leviticus? A good place to start is the truth that the Bible is inspired by God. God speaks to us through it; guiding us, challenging us and helping us to live His way. The real question is not whether the Bible is important and relevant, but how we interpret it in a way that is faithful to the person of Jesus – the focus of the whole book.

THINK

How can we understand what God wants to say to us through a passage from the Bible? Is it enough to just read the words on the page? What else can we consider?

READ: HEBREWS 4:12–16

KEY VERSE v12

'For the word of God is alive and powerful. It is sharper than the sharpest two-edged sword, cutting between soul and spirit ... It exposes our innermost thoughts and desires.'

'A GOOD SAMARITAN.' 'A mass Exodus.' 'A Judas.' 'No rest for the wicked.' There is something about the words of the Bible which lodges in our minds and hearts, as individuals and as a society. There's something about the Bible that registers with us, no matter which culture or era we read it in.

The Bible is hugely relevant to us – uncomfortably so at times. God has a way of speaking through the Bible to challenge us on very specific things in our lives. It's true that the newest parts of the Bible were written nearly 2,000 years ago, but the truths and principles within the pages speak to people's hearts just as directly now as when the words were written. It's almost as if the book itself is alive as God breathes His life into it, making it powerful, inspiring, challenging and uplifting.

But a word of caution: the Bible contains enormous power, but it gains its power from God. So the Bible is not the end in itself but something which points us towards God and inspires us to worship Him. The Bible is the means by which we understand the God we worship and let Him guide us.

PRAY

Thank God for the ways in which He speaks to us and inspires us through the Bible. Ask that He will use it to reveal more of Himself to you.

TUES 17 JUN

READ:
2 PETER 1:12–21

KEY VERSES
vv20–21

'Above all, you must realize that no prophecy in Scripture ever came from the prophet's own understanding ... No, those prophets ... spoke from God.'

SO HOW DOES that work? How can the Bible have been simultaneously written by God and people? Some people find this idea confusing. Others write it off as nonsense, without even really thinking about it. Was God leaning over the writers' shoulders as they put pen to papyrus? Or were these guys just puppets, with God controlling their writing hands?

However it happened, God prompted each of the Bible's 40-or-so writers to record what they had seen, heard and experienced of life and God's words and actions. God let each of these writers use his or her own skill, perspectives and personalities to do that, but inspired them as they wrote. In this way, although the Bible was written by human beings (and only a fraction of it contains words explicitly spoken by God), God communicates His truth through these words.

I doubt whether God dictated where every last comma of the Bible should go, but I wholeheartedly believe that God can and does speak to us through all of it. So the Bible carries real authority. Let's read it with respect and admiration for the God who inspires it.

CHALLENGE

Do you take the Bible seriously? As you read it, remember who inspires it and expect God to challenge you and guide you.

READ: LEVITICUS 19:11–22

KEY VERSE
v19

'Do not mate two different kinds of animals. Do not plant your field with two different kinds of seed. Do not wear clothing woven from two different kinds of thread.'

AS I'M WRITING this, I'm looking at my feet and seeing that my trainers have fabric on the outside and leather inside. Does that mean I'm disobeying God? Is anybody who wears leather elbow patches on their tweed jacket in danger of the fires of hell? Well, obviously not. But this is an example of a verse which non-Christians sometimes use to argue that the Bible is irrelevant. If we ignore this commandment, why should we take any notice of commandments which appear alongside it? What makes the Bible's teaching on sex and money, for example, any more relevant than the two-different-threads thing?

Some of the Bible's teachings are rooted in the time and culture in which they were written. (For example, Leviticus was written for a nation who spent 40 years in the desert. In that environment, ropey clothing would have fallen apart.) But still, the entire Bible has something to teach us. Even the random stuff about different kinds of cloth tells us that God can be gloriously practical in His guidance. He cares about every single area of our lives. This is good news, but also a challenge. If God really cares about everything we do, there's no area of our lives where compromising, or ignoring Him, is OK.

THINK

Are there any teachings from the Bible which you tend to explain away, rather than obey?

READ:
GENESIS 1:1–31

KEY VERSE
v3

'Then God said, "Let there be light," and there was light.'

DID GOD REALLY create the world in six literal 24-hour days? This line of thought leaves us with a world that's approximately 6,000 years old, hence a 'Young Earth'. However, geological evidence and the fossil record put the age of the earth at around 4.5 billion years. How do we explain the difference between the two figures?

Many today believe that this passage was not meant to be taken literally, that instead it takes the form of an epic poem. This idea suggests that the 'six days' is poetic language, representing 'six ages' or 'six periods of time', which could explain the difference between the figures. On the other hand, many believe that it should be taken literally, and that we shouldn't try to fit God's work into our limited understanding – there are many things of God that we cannot comprehend as humans.

What we do know is that Genesis conveys that God is the Almighty Creator – that He, not any pagan god or random explosion is to be credited with creating the universe. We should take this truth absolutely seriously. But we must be open to the possibility that the Earth might be more than 6,000 years old.

CHALLENGE

The timescale of creation and the age of the earth are complex issues. Look into this debate further, exploring both points of view, and draw your own conclusions.

READ: GENESIS 3:1–19

KEY VERSE
vv6–7

'So she took some of the fruit and ate it. Then she gave some to her husband ... At that moment their eyes were opened, and they suddenly felt shame at their nakedness.'

I KEEP A bowl of sugar in my kitchen, next to the kettle. It's helpful when I'm making tea. When he thinks I'm not looking, my four-year-old son will sometimes take a spoon from the drawer and help himself from the sugar bowl. He knows he's not supposed to do it. He knows it's bad for him. But he does it anyway.

Inside each of us there is a natural tendency to be drawn to forbidden things – things that harm ourselves and others. We have a natural tendency towards, for want of a better word, sin. (More on this in August.) And our sin makes us ashamed, alienates us from God and damages our relationships with each other.

With the story of the Fall, the sticking point comes when people ask whether we take it literally. And as with the creation account, it's debatable whether it's historical or figurative. So explore this for yourself. There are many debates out there, with good arguments for each side.

But debates aside, we should absolutely take seriously the truth that it highlights: we are all flawed, foolish, self-destructive people, in dire need of a Saviour.

THINK

What does the story of Adam and Eve say to you about human nature? What does it tell you about God?

WEEKEND

21/22 JUN

READ:

GENESIS 5:1–27

KEY VERSE

v27

'Methuselah lived 969 years, and then he died.'

THE LONGEST-LIVED PERSON since modern records began was a French woman who died in 1997 at the age of 122 years and 164 days. Life expectancy does seem to be increasing these days, largely thanks to better diet and healthcare, but people still generally count themselves lucky if they live into their 80s. So with that kind of background, the idea of someone living for nearly 1,000 years seems more than a little far-fetched. Methuselah and the others in this chapter provide more ammunition for people who label the Bible as 'unbelievable'.

So how do we explain Methuselah and his 969 years of life? Perhaps this chapter is founded on a different understanding of periods of time, with a 'year' actually representing something far shorter. Or maybe, since this is a genealogy, the name of each man stands as a representation of the lifespan of his whole family. Neither of these theories holds much water though. Experts don't really give much credence to either. As crazy as it might sound, the most likely explanation is that Methuselah truly did live for 969 years! It is worth noting that many civilisations have records of surprisingly long lives in the distant past. So just maybe we can take this passage from Genesis at face value.

In any case, in the next chapter, God limits people's lifespan to 120 years (see Genesis 6:3), which is almost exactly the same as the longest life on record. And if someone's greatest objection to believing the Bible is Methuselah's unusually long life, that's hardly a watertight argument against the whole book!

PRAY

Ask for God's help in understanding the parts of the Bible which seem a little strange and for His wisdom in noticing which parts are important and which are less so.

MON 23 JUN

READ: JOSHUA 10:1–15

KEY VERSE v13

'So the sun stood still and the moon stayed in place until the nation of Israel had defeated its enemies.'

SO GOD MADE the sun stand still ... Surely that didn't really happen. I mean, things get exaggerated all the time in the stories of ancient heroes. Surely that's what's happened with this episode from the life of Joshua. More than likely, it just *felt* as if the day was lasting longer than usual because of the intensity of the battle. We can't seriously be expected to believe this story, can we?

But hang on a minute. Even if this story is exaggerated, that doesn't mean it's not at least based on truth. And let's not forget that God is the one who created the sun in the first place. If we accept that, we must accept that He's capable of making the sun stand still, if He wants to. Just because it's extraordinary doesn't mean it's impossible.

There's an important principle at stake here. If we dismiss out of hand everything in the Bible which is outside of our normal experience, we gouge the heart out of it. The Bible is the story of salvation – God's power breaking into human experience to give us hope, security and peace. If we assume that miracles cannot be part of that story, we're robbing God of His power and reducing the Bible to a collection of meaningless fables.

CHALLENGE

Are there any parts of the Bible which you find difficult to believe? Why is that? Do you need to think again about any of this?

READ:
LUKE 23:26–43

KEY VERSE
vv32–33

'Two others, both criminals, were led out to be executed with him ... And the criminals were also crucified – one on his right and one on his left.'

A GOOD FEW people think the Bible is full of contradictions. It's true that there are some passages which appear to have inconsistencies. But 'contradictions'?

Today's reading highlights an example. Luke mentions two criminals who are crucified alongside Jesus. One of them insults Jesus, the other responds entirely differently. But in their versions of the same events, Matthew and Mark say that both criminals insulted Jesus, John doesn't mention the criminals at all and only Luke mentions a criminal being saved as he dies. Does that mean the writers are contradicting each other?

Imagine that you and three friends went to a party. A few days later, someone asks each of you to write down your version of what happened. Of course, all of you would write slightly different versions of events. You might put things in a slightly different order. One or two of you might mention things that the others had forgotten about or just didn't think were worth mentioning. Put together, your accounts would build up a rounded picture of what really happened at the party. In a similar way, we can argue that the gospels do not contradict each other. Rather, they work together to build a fuller picture of Jesus' life, death and resurrection.

THINK

How would you respond to someone who claimed the Bible is full of contradictions?

READ:
PROVERBS 26:1–12

KEY VERSE
vv4–5

'Don't answer the foolish arguments of fools, or you will become as foolish as they are. Be sure to answer the foolish arguments of fools, or they will become wise in their own estimation.'

MORE TODAY ON the 'is the Bible full of contradictions' issue. And actually, verses 4–5 do contradict each other. There are reasons for that contradiction. The Proverbs are short, punchy, memorable phrases which comment on the realities of life, faith and relationships. And one of the realities to which the Proverbs point is that life is complex and unpredictable. For example, it's sometimes hard to tell how a person will respond to something you have to say. Yes, the man who wrote these verses is contradicting himself, but he's doing that on purpose. He's drawing our attention to life's complexity.

There are passages from the Bible which we need to hold in tension with others. For example, we must grapple with the implications of the Old Testament teaching, 'an eye for an eye' (Lev. 24:19-20) and Jesus urging us to turn the other cheek (Matt. 5:39). But the contradictions in Proverbs don't undermine the Bible. In fact they make it more down-to-earth and authentic.

PRAY

Lord God, thank You for understanding how complex and unpredictable life can be. Thank You for being with us in that complexity and helping us when we're confused. Amen.

READ:
JOB 40:15–24

THURS 26 JUN

KEY VERSE
v15

'Take a look at Behemoth, which I made, just as I made you.'

I'M WRITING THESE words just two days after a new species of dinosaur was discovered in America, in the desert of Utah. Nasutoceratops is a member of the triceratops family, but has a huge nose and unusually long horns. Experts say it is unlike anything they have seen before. Dinosaurs are fascinating creatures and there's overwhelming evidence for their existence. So how come the Bible doesn't mention them?

Well, there's a difference between the Bible not mentioning dinosaurs and it actively arguing that they never existed. The Bible isn't like a science textbook. It doesn't set out to describe every species which ever existed and exactly *how* they came into being. It focuses on the *why* of the whole thing: God as their Creator. And on the other hand, maybe the Bible does mention dinosaurs after all. The description of 'Behemoth' in Job 40 is uncannily similar to a large dinosaur. And in a similar way, Leviathan (mentioned in the next chapter and in Psalm 74) could be a plesiosaur – a prehistoric aquatic reptile.

CHALLENGE

Do a bit of research into prehistoric life. It's fascinating stuff! If you've got a friend who knows a bit about this, pick their brains.

FRI 27 JUN

READ:
PSALM 55:16–19

KEY VERSE
v17

'Morning, noon, and night I cry out in my distress, and the LORD hears my voice.'

IN THE LAST couple of weeks, we've covered a lot of ground on the Bible. We've looked at whether it's reliable, believable and authoritative and how we respond to some of its apparent contradictions. Let's move on now and think about prayer for a bit. Sceptics often ask how we know that prayer makes any kind of difference. What makes us think that praying is anything more than words spoken into the air? Studies of hospital patients suggest that those who are prayed for recover more quickly and more fully than those who are not. But a sceptic could argue that this is down to the power of positive thinking.

The most powerful evidence that God hears our prayers is our own experiences. I could tell you about my friend, Steve, who had a broken wrist, prayed, went to the hospital to arrange a date for an operation and found that the break was healed. Or Fraser who was suffering from severe M.E., prayed and heard God speak to him, reassuring him that He was with him. We might feel like our prayers are bouncing off the ceiling at times, but God truly is with us and truly is listening when we pray. We might only see God's involvement in a hard situation in hindsight, but He is there, even if it doesn't feel like it.

PRAY

Thank God for always being with you. Ask Him to help you to keep trusting Him, even when life gets tough and confusing.

WEEKEND 28/29 JUN

READ:
GENESIS 1:26–31

KEY VERSE
V26

'Then God said, "Let us make human beings in our image, to be like us."'

1
2
3
4
5
6
7

CREATION PT2

IN THE FIRST section of our series on 'Creation', we talked about how incredible the world is and how amazing God must be for putting it together. During the next couple of weeks, we'll investigate how God created us, who we are because of that, and how we can use our God-given creativity to worship Him.

The first thing the Bible teaches us about who we are is that God made us to be like Him. This doesn't mean we're perfect, but it does mean that we have the ability to show love, wisdom, justice and truth, just as

7

CONTINUED»

CONTINUED

God does. So, we should do what we can to show those qualities. We should also keep in mind that the people around us are made in God's image too. Because of that, we must respect them – even if we don't like them. Also, when God says, 'Let us make human beings in our image', it shows that we're made in the image of God the Father, Jesus and the Holy Spirit. God models relationship by being three Persons in one God. In the same way, we're created to be in meaningful relationships with other people and with God. We're not supposed to go through life all on our own.

And one final thing: if God the Creator made us to be like Him, surely that means we are naturally creative too. In the next few days, we'll think about what that might mean.

THINK

How can you show the godly qualities of love, wisdom, justice and truth? How will knowing that other people are made in God's image affect how you treat them? How can you make your relationships with your friends and family stronger and more meaningful?

READ:
PSALM 139:1–18

KEY VERSE
v13

'You made all the delicate, inner parts of my body and knit me together in my mother's womb.'

WHEN I WAS a kid, I used to enjoy putting together Airfix kits. (Just in case you've never experienced the joy of an Airfix kit, it includes a load of bits of plastic, which, when put together properly, form a scale model of an aircraft, ship, etc.) My problem was that I was – and still am – a bit clumsy. I'd end up with hardened lumps of glue all over the model. I'd snap the delicate parts or stick them onto the model in slightly the wrong place. And when it came to painting the plane I was making, things really started to go wrong! By the time I'd finished, the model still looked like an aeroplane, but if you compared what I'd produced with the picture on the box, you'd be pretty disappointed.

Fortunately, God doesn't work like this. He isn't clumsy and doesn't make mistakes. When He puts each of us together, He takes care and effort over it, and He knows every last detail about us. And unlike the Airfix kit, God doesn't need to copy a picture on a box. He uses incredible variety in creating our looks, our skills and our personalities. God loves each of us so much that He makes each of us completely unique – a one-off, never to be repeated.

PRAY

Creator God, thank You for making me, me! Thank You for caring about even the smallest details of who I am. Thank You for loving me enough to make me completely unique. Amen.

READ:
JEREMIAH 1:4–10

KEY VERSE
v5

'I knew you before I formed you in your mother's womb.'

GOD KNOWS YOU better than anyone else in the world does. In fact, He even knows you better than you know yourself. Before you were born, before your mum realised she was pregnant, before God even started putting you together, He knew everything about you. When life gets hard, when other people just don't seem to understand us, isn't it comforting to know that God loves us, created us and knows us inside out?

What's more, God has plans for you. And because He knows you so well, His plans for you are perfect. God creates each of us with different skills and personalities and, if we stick to God's plans, we can use our skills and personalities to achieve brilliant things for Him.

Sometimes God will ask us to do things that scare us. For example, Jeremiah's job was to tell his countrymen that they'd turned away from God and to warn them that they were heading for severe consequences because of that! But God will never ask us to do something that we can't do, with His help. And, whatever happens, the God who knows you, created you and loves you is always with you (v8).

THINK
How does it make you feel to know that God knows you better and more deeply than anyone else?

READ:
2 CORINTHIANS 5:14–18

WED 2 JUL

KEY VERSE v17

'... anyone who belongs to Christ has become a new person. The old life is gone; a new life has begun!'

IT'S YOUR FIRST day at school. Your shirt is spotless. Your tie is neat. Your shoes are shiny. How long does your uniform stay that way? After a day or two of running around in the playground, spilling your dinner, enjoying messy art lessons and generally fooling around, you're likely to look a bit grubby. Your mum or dad do the best they can to get the muck out of your shirt, polish your shoes and undo the knots in your tie, but your actions have had an effect. You only really look smart again when you get a new uniform!

When God created humans He made us in His image – excellent! But there was a problem. We messed up. And the selfish choices we make now take us away from God. It's as though our lives get covered in muck that makes it impossible for us to get close to a holy and spotless God. God's solution is amazing. He doesn't try to clean up our old life. He gives us a new one! Because Jesus died and rose again, we can receive His new life. If we follow Jesus, our old life is dead, but we get an exciting, fresh, new life instead. God doesn't just create us once. If we give Him control of our lives, He recreates us!

CHALLENGE

Have you taken up God's offer of a new life? If not, why not do so now? Say sorry to God for the selfish choices which take you away from Him, and ask Him to give you new life in Jesus.

READ:
JAMES 1:16–18

KEY VERSE
v17

'Whatever is good and perfect comes down to us from God our Father, who created all the lights in the heavens.'

WHAT ARE YOU thankful for? Your iPad? That new pair of shoes? The school holidays coming up? Or perhaps life's not good at the moment, and it's difficult to think of anything to be thankful for. If we really think about it, we all have loads to be thankful for, however we feel. Just having somewhere to live, food to eat and clothes to wear are huge blessings, and so many of us have so much more than that. Families, friends, health, the chance of an education – the list goes on, and most of us will have all of these.

It's important to be grateful for the good things we have, but it's also important to remember where these things come from. Anything that's good comes from God. He's the Creator and Provider of everything good, and He always will be. He's been a Creator and Provider from the beginning, and He doesn't change. Because He loves us so much, He keeps creating good things and providing them for us. Anything we have that's good is a gift from the God who loves us.

THINK
Make a list of all the good things in your life. Then thank God for each of these things.

READ: LAMENTATIONS 3:19–24

KEY VERSE
v23

'Great is his faithfulness; his mercies begin afresh each morning.'

THE MOJAVE DESERT, in the Southwest United States, is one of the most inhospitable places on the planet. Temperatures there can reach up to 56.6°C and in the driest years rainfall can be less than five centimetres a year (compared to up to 50 metres a year in parts of Britain). And yet, this hostile environment is the only place in which you will find the Joshua tree. Despite the extreme heat and lack of water, the Joshua tree thrives there. How is this possible? It's because of the tree's deep and extensive root system. The Joshua tree's roots can grow up to 11 metres long in order to find water deep underground. Because the roots are deep enough, the tree can thrive in a seriously harsh environment.

What helps you thrive when life seems harsh? If your roots are deep into God, He can keep you strong and growing, however hot things get. Even if everything else looks bleak, one thing never changes. God is with us. He is faithful, and His love and mercy never run out. It's as if God renews them every day. Whatever happens, you can always trust God to love you and stay with you.

PRAY

Lord, thank You that Your love and mercy are new every morning. Help me to grow deep roots into You, so that I'll stay strong, whatever happens. Amen.

WEEKEND

5/6 JUL

READ:

EXODUS 31:1–11

KEY VERSE

v6

'... I have given special skill to all the gifted craftsmen so they can make all the things I have commanded you to make.'

ERIC LIDDELL WAS a gifted athlete and passionate about sport. At the 1924 Olympics, he won a gold medal in the 400 metres and a bronze in the 200 metres. On his return to his native Scotland, Eric was hailed as a hero. But there were some who were surprised that he was interested in athletics at all. Eric was passionate about running, but he was also passionate about following Jesus. Surely running was just frivolous – a waste of time for a man who wanted to live as a Christian? Eric answered his critics simply: 'I believe that God made me for a purpose, but He also made me fast. And when I run, I feel His pleasure.'

God creates each of us with unique skills and abilities. For Eric Liddell, this meant an ability to run fast. For Bezalel and Oholiab, it meant all kinds of skills in arts and crafts. I wonder what skills God has given you? Perhaps you're great at science or gifted at languages. Maybe you're a musician or a dancer. Maybe God's simply made you wise. If God's created you with a skill, it's important to use it. For a start, it's a way of saying 'Thank You' to God for what He's given you. Also, when we use our gifts, it points other people towards God. Eric Liddell made it clear that God had made him fast. Bezalel and Oholiab used their skills to create a tabernacle, a place where people would be inspired to worship God.

We shouldn't be embarrassed to use our God-given abilities. In fact, it brings Him glory when we use what He's given us.

THINK

What skills has God given you? How can you use your skills to point other people towards Him?

READ: COLOSSIANS 3:16–17

KEY VERSE v17

'... whatever you do or say, do it as a representative of the Lord Jesus ...'

AN AMBASSADOR REPRESENTS his home country, while living in another nation. He communicates his country's interests to the country in which he lives, and whatever he says or does reflects on his home country. Of course, this is a big responsibility. If the ambassador says or does something careless or irresponsible everyone will think less of his country because of it. But it's a real opportunity too. If the ambassador relates well to the people around him and handles difficult situations skilfully, it makes his country look good and really improves the relationship between the two nations.

Today's verses tell us that we're Jesus' ambassadors. We represent Jesus to the people around us. (Remember, Genesis 1:26 tells us that we're created to be like Jesus too.) This is a responsibility, because all we say and do reflects on Jesus and on other Christians. But it's an amazing opportunity too. If we speak and act remembering that we're ambassadors of Jesus, anything we do can be an act of worship to Him and show other people how great He is. Whether we're studying, dancing, playing football or doing the washing up, we can do all these things in a way that brings glory to God.

CHALLENGE

Change one thing in how you speak or act, so that you will represent Jesus better.

READ: PSALM 33:1–3

KEY VERSE v1

'Let the godly sing for joy to the LORD ...'

GOD IS OUR Creator. He created us in painstaking detail, making each of us unique, with unique skills. And He sustains us, keeping us going and giving us the good things we need, day by day. If that isn't enough, if we choose to follow Him, He recreates us, dealing with our sin and giving us a new life. God is an amazing Creator – not just in how He put together the world around us, but in how He treats us too.

When we begin to grasp what God has done for us, it should make us feel good about ourselves, because it's obvious how much He loves us. But more to the point, what God has done for us should inspire us to worship Him. We can respond with joy, and praise God for being so good to us.

Over the next three days, we're going to look at a few verses from Psalm 33 in some detail. Our key verse today, verse 1, mentions singing – and that's a great way to worship, but it's not the only way. In everything we do and say, we can show God that we're grateful for how much He loves us and how much He's done for us.

PRAY

Spend some time now thanking God for what He's done for you, and praising Him for being so amazing.

READ:
PSALM 33:1–3

KEY VERSE
v3

'Sing a new song of praise to him; play skillfully on the harp, and sing with joy.'

WE MENTIONED YESTERDAY that worshipping God doesn't just mean singing. So we shouldn't make the mistake of thinking that if we don't like singing, we can't worship God. Singing worship songs is great, but anything we do can be an act of worship, if our attitude is right. What's more, when we get together to worship God, it's brilliant to do something new. The psalm says: 'Sing a new song ...'. Perhaps we could also say: 'Dance a new dance' or 'Paint a new painting'.

When God made us, He made us just like Him. So, because He's amazingly creative, we must be creative too! We can use our God-given creativity to worship Him, and when we do, it brings a whole new dimension to our time with God. Worship becomes more exciting and vibrant for us – and just maybe it becomes more exciting for God, too! There are so many ways in which we can express ourselves to God: just some of which include photography, dance, sculpture, poetry, even silence. Oh, and music, of course!

THINK

God has made you creative. How can you and your friends use that creativity to express yourselves to God? How can you do something new as you worship Him?

READ: PSALM 33:3–5

KEY VERSE
v5

'He loves whatever is just and good; the unfailing love of the LORD fills the earth.'

GOD LOVES US! I hope you already know that. More than likely, you've heard people say that quite a few times. Often, just a quick look at the world around us and the good things in our lives confirms that God is with us, and that His love does, indeed, fill the earth! This might not always be obvious, however, particularly when we're suffering, but even then, God's promise holds true – He is always with us.

But there's a challenge coupled with that truth. If God is good and fair and loving, then we need to show that to other people. If we accept that God created us to be like Him, we should love justice, like He does. In fact, if we show God's love and justice to other people, this is part of our worship.

God loves it when we do something that's good and fair. Acting to help someone who feels left out or forgotten is a way for us to tell God that we think He's amazing – just in the same way as singing a worship song is.

CHALLENGE

Do something today to show someone that God loves them or to make sure that they are treated fairly. For example, go and do the washing up for your elderly neighbour, talk to the guy in your class or at college whom everyone else ignores, or give some of your money to charity.

READ:
ACTS 4:8–22

KEY VERSE
v20

'We cannot stop telling about everything we have seen and heard.'

A FEW YEARS ago, I got married. This was a really exciting thing for my wife and me, and in the run-up to the wedding we talked to all our friends about how brilliant it was. When you've got a piece of news that's this good, you just can't keep it to yourself. More importantly, we invited all our friends to come to the wedding and celebrate with us. When something amazing happens, you don't just want other people to hear about it, you want them to experience it for themselves.

Peter and John had seen and experienced that God was amazing. He'd done so much for them that they simply couldn't stop telling people about Him. Even when people tried to shut them up, they kept talking because they wanted everyone around them to hear about God and experience for themselves how good He is.

Our response should be the same. If we truly grasp how amazing, how creative and how surprising God is, and appreciate everything He has done for us, we won't be able to help telling people around us. And we'll not only want them to hear about God, we'll want them to get to know and experience Him for themselves.

PRAY

Lord, You are amazing! Thank You for being so good to me and to the world. Help me to see more and more how amazing You are – and fire me up to tell other people about You. Amen.

READ:
1 CORINTHIANS 13:1–13

KEY VERSE V4

'Love is patient and kind. Love is not jealous or boastful or proud ...'

PT2 DATING
GODLY DATING

BACK IN MAY, we started to explore the topic of dating and what the Bible might have to say on this relatively modern phenomenon. We have found that God designed us to be in relationship with others, whether romantic or otherwise and that He wants to guide us in handling relationships wisely. Another key theme we can draw from the Bible is that God shows us how to love others. If we want to know how best to love other people, then the Bible has a lot to tell us. In the next fortnight we will focus on how we can ensure

CONTINUED▶▶

CONTINUED

that we behave in a loving and God-honouring way, in romantic relationships in particular.

Love is powerful. Not only does it have the power to deeply affect our emotions, but our love can have a profound, even physical, effect on others. I remember reading once about a baby who had been stillborn. As his parents cradled him in their arms to say their last goodbyes, however, he started to breathe and show signs of life. Amazingly, this baby who had been declared dead was now alive. The loving words and touch of his parents had stirred his vital organs to begin working.

If you've ever been to a church wedding, then the chances are that you've heard the verses in today's passage before. These words reiterate that love is powerful. They also make us stop and reflect on what actions are loving. Think for a few minutes about the people who love you. How do you know that they love you? In what ways do they express their love? Are there ever times when you doubt their love? Why?

THINK

How do you show love to those around you? Do you need to make more effort in this? How can you take on Paul's words in 1 Corinthians 13 and act on them?

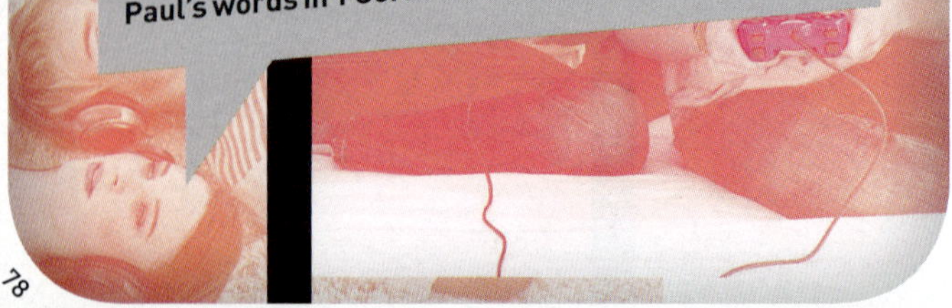

READ: ECCLESIASTES 7:26

KEY VERSE v26

'I discovered that a seductive woman is a trap more bitter than death. Her passion is a snare ...'

WHEN I ASKED you yesterday to think of different ways in which people express love, did you think of any physical expressions of love? Physical affection is one of those important ways we show our love for others. Right from the start of life, a baby experiences her parents' love with how they hold her. Babies who are starved of this loving touch are apparently seriously disadvantaged. Their physical and mental development may be stunted because of it.

Perhaps the ultimate physical expression of love is 'making love' or sex. Some people seem to get the impression that sex is in some way inherently bad. But this is not the case! In fact, sex is part of God's creation – He invented it! So, why is sex sometimes talked about as if it is dangerous, such as in today's key verse?

Think about fire. It has a lot of valuable and important uses. It is not essentially bad. However, imagine you find a small child playing with fire. You would rightly be very worried. Most toddlers are not capable of using fire responsibly. In the wrong hands, fire becomes dangerous. We could say the same thing about sex. It's good, important and very enjoyable, but if we use it irresponsibly, we can easily get hurt, and hurt others.

PRAY

Thank God for the gift of sex. Ask for His wisdom in using this gift in the way He intended.

READ:
1 THESSALONIANS 4:3–8

KEY VERSE
v3

'God's will is for you to be holy, so stay away from all sexual sin.'

YESTERDAY WE EXPLORED the idea that sex is good but can also be dangerous. Most Christians therefore see sex as best saved for marriage. Probably the next question is, 'How far is too far in a dating relationship?' Or is that looking at it the wrong way? When we ask the question, 'How far is too far?' maybe what we're really asking is, 'How far can I go before I'm in trouble with God?'

If I built a huge bonfire and then asked you to soak your left arm in petrol and see how close you could get your arm to the fire before it caught light, would you do it? Probably not! But when it comes to sex we ask, 'How far is too far? How far can I go without getting burned?'

God's will is for us to be holy. In every area of our lives, He wants us to be pure and godly, even when that goes against what everyone else seems to be doing. As part of this, God wants us to stay away from sexual sin. So, rather than asking how far it is OK to go in our physical relationships, perhaps we should be asking, 'How can I stay pure and honour God in this relationship?'

CHALLENGE

Many people are still technically virgins, but couldn't be said to be living in a pure and holy way. Do you need to change your attitude on this? Is there anything you need to say sorry to God for, and receive His forgiveness?

READ: SONG OF SONGS 2:1–17

KEY VERSE v7

'Promise me, O women of Jerusalem … not to awaken love until the time is right.'

MOST PEOPLE WHO haven't read a lot of the Bible would probably perceive it to be anti-sex. But this is certainly not the case! Song of Songs uses a lot of imagery but, even so, it is not difficult to work out what the gist of it is. It describes an intense love and attraction between a man and a woman, with a clear physical element to their relationship. Having read Song of Songs, we can see that sex is not inherently wrong; in this context it's good! (In fact, the couple's expressions of *how* good are enough to make you blush!) However, the book does underline that there is a right time and place for acting on a physical attraction.

In today's key verse, we are warned 'not to awaken love until the time is right' (Songs 2:7). What does that mean in the physical sense? Well, we need to decide what boundaries we'll set up in our physical relationships. Ask yourself what do you want to save for marriage? How can you honour this person and God with your actions? Whether or not you are dating somebody at the moment, these are important things to consider.

CHALLENGE

Working out your boundaries ahead of time will help you stick to them. What might it mean for you 'not to awaken love until the time is right'?

READ:
PROVERBS 31:10–12, 25–31

KEY VERSE
v30

'Charm is deceptive, and beauty does not last; but a woman who fears the LORD will be greatly praised.'

EVERY YEAR AT Christmas my husband plays a trick on somebody. He offers some poor unsuspecting person a delicious chocolate truffle. When they bite into it, however, they find that it is a chocolate-covered Brussels sprout.

We can often be fooled by first impressions. If you had to define what makes somebody attractive, what would you say? A perfect figure, a confident attitude and stylish clothes will all get people's attention. But what really matters in a person is far deeper than that. Whether you're male or female, it's your character that really counts.

Rather than get carried away with first impressions, take some time to think about what really counts in a boyfriend/girlfriend. What do you have in common with this person? Do you share important values and priorities? Will this person help you to maintain a healthy focus on God and His plans for your life? Is this person attractive on the surface but, frankly, ugly underneath?

THINK

What would God say about what you look for in a potential boyfriend/girlfriend? And on the other hand, what impression do you give other people? Are you more concerned with looking good than with becoming more like Jesus?

READ: PROVERBS 2:12–22

KEY VERSE
v16

'Wisdom will save you from the immoral woman, from the seductive words of the promiscuous woman.'

I KNEW SOMEBODY who was madly in love with a girl he wanted to marry. However, he wanted to seek the advice of people he trusted, such as his church leaders, before he popped the question. To his disappointment, when he asked their advice, he didn't get the answer he wanted. They told him to wait a while longer before proposing. My friend was so unhappy with this advice that he chose to ignore it. He went ahead and proposed to his girlfriend and the church leaders were not invited to the wedding.

All too often, we can be like this. We want wise advice from other people, but we want their wisdom to be something that's easy to hear. Proverbs highlights the importance of wisdom in helping us make the right choices about our relationships. Bad decisions in this area of life can have devastating consequences. We need to be disciplined and show real wisdom when it comes to dating. Remember to guard your heart, as it's so easy to get carried away by our emotions. We'll sometimes have to choose between what's right and what's appealing.

PRAY

Ask for God's wisdom for making decisions on romantic relationships. Ask Him to help you make the right decision, when the wrong decision is a more attractive option.

WEEKEND
19/20 JUL

READ:
PROVERBS 22:24–25

KEY VERSE
v24
'Don't befriend angry people or associate with hot-tempered people ...'

THERE ARE SOME people I know who bring out the worst in me. When I am around them I can feel myself getting increasingly tense and grumpy. With others, I'm more inclined than usual to start gossiping! Proverbs 22 reminds us that hanging around with the wrong sort of people can have a negative effect on our own personality. It's so true that when we hang around with someone who is always grumpy and negative, their attitude rubs off on us. This is not to say we shouldn't help someone who is going through a difficult time and whose emotions are obviously impacted by this, but we should always be aware of the effect others are having on us.

Thankfully, I can also think of people in my life who bring out the best in me. They encourage me when I'm down, challenge me when I am doing the wrong thing and spur me on to serve God and others. They share God's wisdom and truth with me and always look out for my best interests. These are the people whom God wants me to be influenced by. And the Holy Spirit is the best influence of all. Galatians 5 tells us that when we allow the Holy Spirit to influence us, He produces 'love, joy, peace, patience, kindness, goodness, faithfulness, gentleness, and self-control' in us (Gal. 5:22–23). The Holy Spirit will not only produce these great traits in us, He will also lead us to the right people and help us deal with those who once influenced us in the wrong way.

THINK

If our purpose in life is to know God and live for Him, then we must look for people who will support us in this. On the other hand, we should be looking to see how we can support others in their own walk with Jesus. How are you doing with those goals at the moment?

READ:
PSALM 4:1–8

KEY VERSE
v4

'Don't sin by letting anger control you. Think about it overnight and remain silent.'

ARGUMENTS FEATURE IN all relationships. In fact, it is something to worry about if you never disagree with someone! What is important is how you deal with your differences when disagreements come up.

Many people home in on the Bible's advice not to let the sun go down on your anger (Eph. 4:26). This is a valuable piece of advice but can, when misinterpreted, lead to more problems. But not letting the sun go down on your anger does not have to mean getting the whole issue sorted out before you go to sleep. I don't know about you but when I'm tired I become irrational and stress about issues I wouldn't normally worry about. This makes it very difficult to sort out any arguments. This is where today's verse comes in handy. To let go of our anger does not necessarily mean sorting out the whole issue.

My mum always tells me that things will look better in the morning and I have come to realise that she's often right. Things that get me worried late at night often seem insignificant once I've had a good night's sleep.

PRAY

Father God, help me to behave in a godly way when I disagree with someone. Help me to be patient and to control my anger. Amen.

READ: GENESIS 13:5–9

KEY VERSE v9

'Take your choice of any section of the land you want, and we will separate.'

WE HAVE ALL heard of divorce proceedings that turn nasty, perhaps amongst people we know or celebrities in the news. One of the divorces that sticks in my mind was between Paul McCartney and Heather Mills a few years ago. I can't get over the huge amounts of money involved in that split.

Whether we like it or not, many of our dating relationships will come to an end. Abram and Lot were uncle and nephew, so certainly weren't in a romantic relationship, but the way in which they parted sets a great example for us.

The disputes had started to break out between Abram and his nephew Lot's people as a result of them 'living so close together' (Gen. 13:6). I am sure we can identify this problem in some of our own relationships with people we are close to. Eventually, Abram and Lot agree that they have to go their own separate ways. What is remarkable is what Abram does next. When we split up with someone, we often look out for our own interests in the situation. We want to benefit as much as possible. But this is not Abram's attitude. He allows Lot to choose the land that he prefers, and agrees to accept what is left.

CHALLENGE

In your relationships, particularly when they come to an end, are you out to get the best for yourself? How can you adopt Abram's attitude when a relationship comes to an end?

READ:
GALATIANS 5:13–15

KEY VERSE
v15

'But if you are always biting and devouring one another, watch out! Beware of destroying one another.'

IT SHOULD COME as no surprise that God commands us to love other people. (After all, God Himself *is* love – 1 John 4:8.) But along with this command come warnings of the negative consequences when we don't love others in the way that we should. In your relationships with others, do you truly love them? Do you build them up to be the best people they can be? What about when you're arguing?

Today's passage warns us against destroying one another. However, as well as destroying one another, we can also do damage to our relationship with God when we leave issues unresolved. In Matthew 5 we read that we cannot come before God with a clear conscience if we are not at peace in our relationships (Matt. 5:23–24).

Conflict is an inevitable part of relationships, but we must be careful even at these times to ensure we behave in a godly way and do our best to love the other person. When we do not deal with issues wisely, there can be severe and damaging consequences.

THINK

Is there somebody with whom you have had a relationship that ended badly? Are there past hurts that have not been resolved? Ask God to help you deal with these issues whether privately in your own heart or by talking things over with the person involved.

READ: PHILIPPIANS 2:1–5

KEY VERSE v2

'... agreeing wholeheartedly with each other, loving one another, and working together with one mind and purpose.'

MY BROTHER AND I are quite skilled at being able to tell what the other is thinking. We are often able to finish each other's sentences, because we each know exactly what is on the other's mind. We hear of twins being like this, having some kind of unusually strong link through their close relationship.

In today's passage, Paul urges us to work 'together with one mind and purpose' (Phil. 2:2). We know that the Bible describes marriage as a husband and wife becoming 'united into one' (Mark 10:8). In our relationships, then, we need to have the same focus and be united in our purpose.

We have thought a lot about choosing the right partner and not being led astray by somebody who is not good for you. However, we also need to be concerned with our own actions and behaviour and whether or not we are a good influence on our partner! This passage emphasises the importance of putting others and their needs first.

PRAY

Lord Jesus, thank You that You were willing to humble Yourself and come to earth to save us. Help us to put others' needs before our own. In our relationships, help us to be united in one purpose, to serve You. Amen.

READ:
1 JOHN 4:7–21

KEY VERSE
v10

'This is real love – not that we loved God, but that he loved us and sent his Son as a sacrifice to take away our sins.'

IF YOU HAD to try and define love, what would you say? There are several words for love in Ancient Greek, all with slightly different meanings. Although we haven't got space to go into all of these today, *eros* and *agape* are perhaps the two most relevant for us to consider. *Eros* is a passionate, often physical love. It is from this word that we get our English word 'erotic'. *Agape* could be described as a sacrificial and unconditional love. You could say it is more of a spiritual love than the physical attraction implied by *eros*.

In your definition of love, did you focus more on one of these kinds of love or did they have an equal balance? Would you be happy to have a dating or marriage relationship that only consisted of one of these types of love or do you think that both are necessary?

In the original Greek of 1 John 4, the word used for 'love' is *agape*. God is the ultimate definition of *agape* love. God calls us to demonstrate *agape* love to everyone, which is a huge challenge to all of us, whether we're in a relationship or not!

CHALLENGE

Spend some time looking back over today's passage and 1 Corinthians 13. Both of these passages give us insights into what *agape* love looks like. How can you reflect *agape* love in your own relationships, whether romantic or otherwise? What changes will you make in light of this?

WEEKEND 26/27 JUL

READ:
ACTS 2:42-47

KEY VERSE
V44

'And all the believers met together in one place and shared everything they had.'

MONEY PT2

IT WOULD BE very difficult not to have noticed that over the last few years the UK, along with a lot of the rest of Europe, has been experiencing something of a financial crisis. The term 'recession' is one that is used on a regular basis, and many people are finding themselves affected by this.

Times like these cause us to tighten our belts and think very carefully about where our money goes, including the different charities and causes that we give to. How should we, as Christians, respond to such a crisis? Is it right for us to reduce our giving? How do

CONTINUED

CONTINUED

we support those who are really going through difficult times financially?

It has always been the case that some have more than others. And in order to counteract this, the early Christians we read about in today's reading chose to live in community, sharing everything they had so no one went without.

It might not be possible for us to live in community in quite the same way, but the Bible still gives insight and instruction as to how we should care for each other in hard times. Over the next couple of weeks we're going to be looking at part of a letter that the apostle Paul wrote to the church in Corinth, whose members were also experiencing tough financial circumstances. This church was full of fairly new Christians who still needed to be taught about giving, so Paul gave them some principles that we too can model in our own giving. These principles can help us (and would have helped the Corinthian Christians) to remember that Jesus is the most generous giver of all.

PRAY

Lord, thank You that You know all that we are going through and the situations in which we find ourselves. Please speak to me about how I can play my part in supporting others. Amen.

READ: 2 CORINTHIANS 8:1-5

KEY VERSE v2

'... they are very poor. But they are also filled with abundant joy, which has overflowed in rich generosity.'

A MEMORY THAT will live on in my mind is the time I spent in a Sudanese village with a small group of Christians. These people had very little and often didn't have enough to eat from day to day. I had been doing some teaching with them and at the end of the course they had made a collection and bought me a beautiful gift. Their joy in giving the gift was very evident, but I knew that for most of them, their giving would mean they would have to go without something else – probably food.

In this part of his letter, Paul is encouraging the church in Corinth to be generous and is using the example of a church in Macedonia, who were experiencing even more difficult times than the Corinthians. The first principle Paul wants them to grasp is that generosity is possible even when your finances are really stretched, and that it's possible to give with joy, even in these circumstances. In the face of severe affliction and extreme poverty, the Macedonian believers responded with joy. How? Because they recognised that God had been generous to them, so they should extend that to others.

CHALLENGE

Is there anyone you know who is struggling financially right now? What will you do to help them? Could you club together with some friends to help this person out?

TUES 29 JUL

READ:
2 CORINTHIANS 8:6-7

KEY VERSE
v7

'Since you excel in so many ways ... I want you to excel also in this gracious act of giving.'

DID YOU KNOW that giving is a spiritual gift? I have a friend who, by her own admission, would say that before she was a Christian she found it very difficult to be generous. She hated being stopped in the street by charity workers trying to raise money for their cause, and felt quite angry that people would expect her to give her hard-earned money away. Today that has all changed. Since becoming a Christian, she has found that she has a real concern for those who are struggling and loves to find ways of helping people out, often without them knowing about it. She would say that God has softened her heart to the needs of others.

In 2 Corinthians, Paul acknowledges that giving doesn't always come easily to people. It doesn't feel natural to want to give money away when times are difficult, but he says this is a gift or a 'ministry' to be exercised. He challenges the Corinthians not to just do this a little bit but to really excel in it. His second principle for them to learn is that giving is a spiritual gift – it is something the Holy Spirit can help them to do.

THINK
Are there people you know who have a great gift of giving? Talk to them about what has helped them to be generous.

READ: 2 CORINTHIANS 8:8-9

KEY VERSE v9

'Though he [Jesus] was rich, yet for your sakes he became poor, so that by his poverty he could make you rich.'

WHEN WE READ about Jesus' life in the Gospels, we find He was born into a humble family, and as an adult didn't seem to have a home of His own or anything much by way of material possessions. However, Paul wants the Christians to remember that that wasn't always the case for Jesus. He left the riches of heaven to come to earth, so that we could be restored and forgiven and experience life in all its fullness.

Paul reminds his readers of the generosity that Jesus showed to them and to us all, both through His life and His death. So when we are generous to others, we remind ourselves and others of Jesus' generosity. Paul tells us: 'Don't do this because you have to. Do it because you want to, because you know that is how God has treated you.'

In a letter to another church, the church in Philippi, Paul picks up this theme and tells us that we should have the same attitude as Jesus. And when we are generous with others, they will be reminded of Him (Phil. 2:5-11).

PRAY

Thank You, Lord, that You gave up the riches of heaven to come and live on earth and to die on the cross to pay my debt. Please let my life reflect my thankfulness to You. Amen.

READ:
2 CORINTHIANS 8:10-12

KEY VERSE
v12

'Whatever you give is acceptable if you give it eagerly. And give according to what you have, not what you don't have.'

PAUL'S FOURTH PRINCIPLE is incredibly practical and immensely freeing! We can be so tempted to compare ourselves to others in a whole number of areas that we forget that God sees us as individuals and knows the situation we are in.

A couple of years ago I went shopping with a friend who earns a lot more money than I do. We ended up in a very expensive shop that sold beautiful handbags. My friend bought a bag and before I knew what I was doing, I had bought one too. As soon as I got home I started regretting my purchase. I realised I was spending according to her budget, not mine. The next day, I took the bag back to the shop!

We all have different amounts of resources available to us, and God doesn't expect us all to give the same. What He is interested in is our heart: are we generous with what we have? Or are we stingy and wanting to hold on to it all for ourselves? Paul's advice to the Corinthians links back to the passage we looked at a few weeks ago about the poor widow who gave just a couple of pennies. In Jesus' eyes she gave much more than the rich people, because to Jesus it's not the amount that matters, it's our willingness to give cheerfully, even when that hurts.

CHALLENGE

Do you give regularly to a charity or to your church?

READ: 2 CORINTHIANS 8:13-15

KEY VERSE v14

'Right now you have plenty and can help those who are in need. Later, they will have plenty and can share with you when you need it.'

A MOMENTOUS DECISION was made in the youth group where I was a volunteer, that the youth room needed some serious revamping. The room was a great size, but was looking very tatty and run-down. A plan was drawn up that would make it a great resource, both for the young people in our church and for others to use. The final cost for all the work that needed doing came in quite high, but, undeterred, the group went about raising the money.

During this process, we heard about a church in Moldova who were in a similar situation, although they didn't really have much of a room to start with. We decided that while we were raising funds for our room, we would also make sure we had enough to build a room for them too.

This is the principle that Paul is applying in these verses. At that moment the church in Corinth had more resources than churches in other places, but the time would come when it would be the other way around. When we have plenty, we have an opportunity to bless others.

THINK

Where in the world is there a need that you know of? How could you use your plenty to help with this need?

WEEKEND
2/3 AUG

READ:
2 CORINTHIANS 9:1-5

KEY VERSE
v2

'In fact, it was your enthusiasm that stirred up many of the Macedonian believers to begin giving.'

GROWING UP, MY sister and I were incredibly competitive with each other. If one learnt how to play the recorder, the other had to learn how to do it better. If one of us could swim 20 lengths, the other had to swim 50. The competition between us led to a certain amount of friction in our relationship. Fortunately, we're a bit more laid back these days and have forgiven each other! But competition isn't always a bad thing; it can sometimes spur us on to do more than we thought. I know that's certainly true of us!

Paul is encouraging the Corinthians in a level of healthy competition with the church in Macedonia, and reminds them that it was because the Macedonians were so inspired by their generosity that they themselves started giving. However, it now seemed that the Macedonians were out-giving the Corinthians and Paul was anxious that the Corinthians wouldn't forget the promise of support that they had made to the church in Jerusalem.

Paul appeals to their pride, pointing out how embarrassing it would be if he were to arrive in Corinth with some people from Macedonia to collect their gift and take it on to the church in Jerusalem, only to find that they didn't have it ready. He really wanted them to honour their promises of support.

CHALLENGE

Have you made promises to other people (or even to yourself) about giving money to support a particular person or cause? Don't just say you'll do it! Now is the time to put your hand in your pocket and give.

READ: 2 CORINTHIANS 9:6-7

KEY VERSE v7

'And don't give reluctantly or in response to pressure. "For God loves a person who gives cheerfully."'

ON THE STREET where I live, we get a lot of people 'cold-calling' at our front doors. I open the door to people from all sorts of different charities, wanting me to sign up to give £2 a month to support some project or other. Without fail, each one will tell me how wonderful my neighbours have been in signing up. I often feel under pressure to give the person on the doorstep what they want, and at times I've done so, but not particularly cheerfully.

Paul is keen that the Corinthians don't find themselves in that place. He says that we should make our own minds up about how much we will give and then do that cheerfully. However, Paul wants them to be aware that a farming principle is also at work in how we live with our money – you will reap what you sow. So, just as you will reap a harvest of tomatoes if you plant tomatoes, if you sow generously you will receive generously. You will see a harvest of people's lives being changed as a result of your generosity.

THINK

Take some time to review the work of a few charities and find out what it is they are raising money for. Is this something you could give to cheerfully?

READ: 2 CORINTHIANS 9:8-10

TUES 5 AUG

KEY VERSE v8

'And God will generously provide all you need. Then you will always have everything you need and plenty left over to share with others.'

JOHN WESLEY WAS a famous preacher whom God used to bring thousands of people to faith in eighteenth century England. Wesley is also known as the man who started the Methodist Church. His name is very well known in Christian circles, but not many people know that Wesley made a lot of money from preaching.

One cold winter's day, he was very challenged by God about how he used his money. He had bought new pictures for his home and had just finished paying for them when the maid arrived, wearing only a thin dress. Wesley wanted to give her some money to buy a coat, but realised that he didn't have any left. From that point on, he resolved to live on £28 a year, no matter how much he earned, and give the rest away. He believed that with increasing income, it shouldn't be a Christian's standard of living that improves, but their standard of giving. Wesley encouraged other Christians to gain all the money they could, so they could do good with it. He also encouraged them to buy only what they really needed. When we buy what we don't need, we then want more things that we don't need. When he died, the only money Wesley had was the change in his pocket.

CHALLENGE

This week, rather than spending money on something for yourself, could you buy something for someone in need?

READ:
2 CORINTHIANS 9:11-13

KEY VERSE
v13

'... they will give glory to God. For your generosity to them ... will prove that you are obedient to the Good News of Christ.'

FOR PAUL, EVERYTHING is linked. The way we behave is clearly linked to what we believe. If we believe that God has been generous to us and given us all things, then we will be quick to be generous to others. We will recognise that all that we have belongs to God and we are simply looking after it for Him.

Martin Luther is quoted as having said that the last part of a person to be converted is their wallet! As we get closer to God and grow in our faith, we will find that our tight grip on money, possessions and other things starts to loosen. Along with this, we will find our motives changing. Whereas we may once have been driven to get as much as we could for ourselves and reluctant to share with others, as the Holy Spirit works in our lives we will find that we want to use what we have to bless others. Paul says this is an indication that you have really understood the good news of Jesus and are living it out. And when you live in this way, it is really pleasing to God because it proves that you are becoming more like Him.

PRAY

God, You have given me so many good things, and most of all You have given Jesus so that I could know You. Please make me more and more like You. Amen.

READ:
2 CORINTHIANS 9:14

KEY VERSE
v14

'And they will pray for you with deep affection because of the overflowing grace God has given to you.'

WHAT WE DO with our money and possessions has the potential for far-reaching effects. Believe it or not, it's often true that the more we are willing to let go, the more we receive. This doesn't always mean receiving more money, but as we give, God will often bless us in other ways. Apart from anything else, we have the privilege of becoming part of God's work in building His kingdom.

For example, I've just finished reading the biography of a young woman who moved to Uganda when she was just 19-years-old, and by the age of 22 had adopted 14 Ugandan children. In the world's eyes, she has given up a good life, a secure future, her education and so much more. Yet, as I read her story, I couldn't help but be struck by how rich her life sounded: not rich in terms of money and possessions, but rich in people who loved her and rich in terms of seeing God at work in the people around her. It's a unique joy to see God transforming people as we invest our time and energy in them. This kind of investment often means we have to sacrifice our own interests, but it can change people's lives, not just in the here and now, but for eternity.

CHALLENGE

Over this coming weekend, read a biography of someone who has given up a comfortable life for the sake of the kingdom of God. Reflect on what you can learn from them.

FRI 8 AUG

READ:
2 CORINTHIANS 9:15

KEY VERSE
v15
'Thank God for this gift too wonderful for words!'

I LOVE CHRISTMAS and birthdays! I love gifts, both receiving them and giving them. I love to see the way people respond to gifts that have been carefully chosen for them, and I feel very thankful for the thought that people have put into gifts for me. Gifts are a key part of our lives but really shouldn't just be reserved for Christmas and birthdays. God has given us a wonderful gift in His Son, Jesus, and it's through Him that we can live to serve God and serve others.

As we come to the end of this part of Paul's letter, he really wants the church in Corinth, and us, to understand that because we have received so much from God, we can be people who love to freely give to others. When we know the truth of the extent of God's love for us, we find things change in us. Our identity and status are no longer found in what we own or in how much money we have; it all becomes about God. Our attitude towards those things changes, not because God says it must, but because it's a natural overflow of His goodness to us.

THINK

Go back over the last two weeks' readings and remind yourself of the principles that Paul sets out about how we think about and use money. How will you put these principles into action?

READ:
ROMANS 8:18–30

KEY VERSE
V26

'... we don't know what God wants us to pray for. But the Holy Spirit prays for us with groanings that cannot be expressed in words.'

PT2
APOLOGETICS 2

I REMEMBER EXACTLY where I was on September 11, 2001. I was in Luton, with about 60 other people, on residential training for my year out. When the news came through about the terrorist attacks at the World Trade Centre and the Pentagon, none of us could quite believe it. We switched on the TV and sat in stunned silence as the horror of what we were seeing began to hit us. The sheer scale of the devastation was impossible to take in: the number of people who had lost their lives, the chaos and destruction in New York, the utter evil in the way

CONTINUED

CONTINUED▶▶

the terrorists went about their task. All of us were Christians, so the obvious response was to pray. But where could we start?

There are times when praying seems incredibly difficult. When we're faced with a tragedy on a personal or even global scale, words often fail us. It's comforting to know that the Holy Spirit prays with us and for us, even in the most extreme circumstances. Through Him, God hears the prayers in our hearts, even if we can't articulate those words. Prayer isn't about saying the right words in the right way. It's just about laying ourselves open before God – being honest about how we're feeling and what's going on in our lives. It's about a relationship with our Father God who created us and loves us. The Holy Spirit helps us to draw closer to God, even when we can't say a word. People often ask whether prayer achieves anything. Maybe that's missing the point. The most important thing about prayer is simply being with God. Any tangible answers to prayer are secondary to that.

PRAY

Spend time with God, being honest about how you're doing and what's on your mind. Don't say a word if you don't want to. Just enjoy being with your Heavenly Father.

READ: JAMES 5:13–18

KEY VERSE v16

'The earnest prayer of a righteous person has great power and produces wonderful results.'

TWO FRIENDS OF mine – a married couple – were desperate for a baby and having real trouble conceiving. They prayed. Nothing happened. They kept praying. Still nothing. They started thinking about medical help in the conception process. They were just about to make a decision when they discovered they were pregnant!

Another couple I know were in a similar situation: desperate for a baby and having no luck in conceiving. They prayed. Nothing happened. They kept praying. Still nothing. They're still wrestling with this situation now. They're still praying, obviously, but also beginning to wonder whether, for reasons they don't understand, God isn't going to bless them with a baby.

From the first couple's experiences, we can see that God can and does answer our prayers. From the second couple's experiences, it's clear that it doesn't always happen like that. I have no idea why. As we struggle with unanswered prayers, we can only remind ourselves that God is infinitely wise and has reasons beyond our understanding. If we choose to trust Him completely, even when life doesn't make sense, we can be in no better place.

THINK

Why do you think God doesn't give us everything we ask for? Think about it and let it lead you into prayer, asking for God's wisdom.

TUES 12 AUG

READ:

JOHN 8:31–47

KEY VERSE
vv31–32

'Jesus said ... "... if you remain faithful to my teachings ... you will know the truth, and the truth will set you free."'

TRUTH CAN BE a bit of a slippery thing. These days, people are happy that what you believe can be 'true for you', while at the same time believing something entirely different themselves. So when Christians claim that Jesus is the truth and that He is true for everyone, we often get a frosty response.

Some truth *is* objective. To take a very extreme example, we all know that the Holocaust happened. There is overwhelming evidence of it, including the experiences of people who survived the death camps. You can't argue that the Holocaust didn't happen and expect to be told, 'Well, that's true for you'. It's a historical fact.

On the other hand, I would argue that chocolate is the best ice cream flavour. For me, that's true. You might think that strawberry is the best flavour. That's true for you and it would be very hard for me to convince you otherwise. It's just a matter of opinion.

Jesus isn't an ice cream. It's not a matter of Him being true for some of us but not others. Jesus made claims about Himself which demand that we choose whether we believe in Him or not. He's either the Son of God or He isn't. It can't be true for me but not for you.

CHALLENGE

Jesus promises that the truth will set us free, but only if we faithfully follow His teaching. So ... are you faithfully following His teaching?

READ: MATTHEW 7:1–5

KEY VERSE v1

'Do not judge others, and you will not be judged.'

IT'S SO SAD to hear someone say they'd love to come to church, but they need to 'sort themselves out' first. Somehow, we're giving people the impression that they need to have every little issue in their lives sorted out before they're acceptable – either to God or to us. Somewhere along the line, we've got ourselves a reputation for being judgmental; for pouncing on shortcomings in other people's lives, while showing no concern for our own weaknesses.

In some cases, this might be down to guilt people feel when doing things they know are wrong. Or perhaps we live in a way that's so obviously godly that others feel they can't measure up to that. Maybe. But whether we like it or not, there are a lot of people who have been judged, criticised and gossiped about by Christians and who have been left angry at us and angry at God because of it. If we have a reputation for being judgmental, we've done a fair amount to deserve it. If we want to win over non-Christians, we must be willing to admit our previous failings in showing God's grace.

THINK

How can we show God's grace and acceptance to other people, even if we don't approve of how they behave? How can we be intolerant of sin but unconditionally accepting of people?

READ:
JOHN 10:1–16

KEY VERSE
v10

'The thief's purpose is to steal and kill and destroy. My purpose is to give them a rich and satisfying life.'

ANOTHER COMMON COMPLAINT about Christianity is that it limits our freedom. God is often thought of as an almighty killjoy who just wants to stop us enjoying ourselves. Nothing could be further from the truth. Jesus assures us that His purpose is to give us a 'rich and satisfying life'. Yes, that includes life after death, but it starts here and now.

If you're a Christian, you're free to stay up all night, do a bungee jump, visit China, get married, see an amazing film, talk to a stranger, ride a horse, climb a mountain, jump off a waterfall, have kids, sip coke while watching the sun go down over the Zambezi River, have a Christmas dinner in June and cycle the length of the British Isles. Following Jesus can and should be an adventure. Yes, there are a few experiences God doesn't want us to have – promiscuous sex, drinking too much and taking drugs, for example – but that's not because He wants to spoil our fun. The things God warns us away from will ultimately harm us if we pursue them.

CHALLENGE
Do you miss opportunities because you're naturally cautious? Pray about it, then take a chance and have an adventure. Or do you rush into risky situations because you're impulsive? Ask God to help you be a little wiser.

READ: PSALM 103:1–13

KEY VERSE
v8

'The LORD is compassionate and merciful, slow to get angry and filled with unfailing love.'

WESTBORO BAPTIST CHURCH are notorious for being about the most unforgiving, ungracious Christians in the world. Based in Topeka, Kansas, members of the church picket the funerals of gay people and soldiers, pronouncing God's judgment on them in terms that would make your eyes water. They don't stop there, either. Jews, Muslims and even Sweden have been targeted with Westboro's abuse. (I mean, Sweden! How could anyone hate Sweden?!) And tragically enough, they believe they are on a mission to spread 'God's hate'. 'God's hate'?!

But before we start feeling smug because we're not as unforgiving as those guys, just spend a minute thinking about the last person who really let you down. Have you forgiven them? Not easy, is it? C.S. Lewis once pointed out that everyone says forgiveness is a lovely idea until they have something to forgive. But although it's far from easy, forgiveness is God's way. In the same way that God has forgiven us, we're called to forgive other people. The best way to counter the view that Christians are unforgiving is, with God's help, to become known for your gracious, forgiving attitude.

PRAY

Ask God to help you forgive. Pray for anyone who's let you down badly and ask for God's help in forgiving them in particular.

WEEKEND

16/17 AUG

READ:
LEVITICUS 18:15–30

KEY VERSE
v22

'Do not practice homosexuality, having sex with another man as with a woman. It is a detestable sin.'

THIS VERSE FROM Leviticus tends to provoke strong reactions. It's often highlighted by those who claim Christians are intolerant. For example, the actor Sir Ian McKellen once tore this page out of a Bible in front of an audience of hundreds, because he felt it was so out of touch with his lifestyle and culture.

On the other extreme, this is the 'go-to' verse for Christians who are outspoken against homosexual behaviour. The thing is, if we oppose homosexual practice based on this single verse, we haven't got a case. Leviticus forbids homosexuality alongside wearing clothes made of two different fabrics (see the Wed 18 Jun reading). If we no longer insist on the one, we can't insist on the other, either. But we don't base it on just this verse. We base it on the broad sweep of what the Bible has to say about what God created human beings to be, from the creation account in Genesis to the teachings against homosexual practice in the New Testament.

So does that make Christians intolerant? Well, actually, yes! We must love and accept everyone, whether or not we approve of how they behave, but we can't endorse homosexual practice if we believe it's wrong. However, it would be misleading to give the impression that Christians are 100% united against homosexual practice. Many Christians, after a lot of thought and prayer, have reached the conclusion that the Bible's teachings against homosexual practice are no longer applicable. So if we're going to decide not to tolerate something, we need to be absolutely sure that we really know what we're talking about and aware that we may not speak for everyone who calls themselves a Christian.

THINK

What do you choose not to tolerate? Why? Do some real thinking, praying and discussing around these issues.

READ:
JAMES 4:1–12

KEY VERSE
v1

'What is causing the quarrels and fights among you? Don't they come from the evil desires at war within you?'

IT'S REALLY SAD when people accuse the Church of being abusive and controlling. A lot of people seem to like Jesus but have a real problem with 'organised religion'. They've got a point. Altogether too many churches are riddled with 'quarrels and fights' over petty issues. And there are churches out there whose leaders are so domineering that anyone who expresses a different opinion gets shouted down or ignored.

This is not the way it should be. Churches are full of people and people are imperfect. So some disagreements and personality clashes will happen. But we should strive to be united under God, to put our selfish agendas to one side, serve one another and pursue God's kingdom. One day, the Church will be made perfect, just as the people in it are made perfect. In the meantime, we shouldn't judge the Church because it's a little rough around the edges. We should see it as God sees it; as the bride of Christ, something beautiful. We should commit ourselves to being part of the bride's makeover – doing everything we can to help the Church become more beautiful.

CHALLENGE

Think of one thing you can do to serve the Church and make it more beautiful. Talk to your friends at church and your church leader. Then put your idea into practice.

READ: PSALM 51:1–19

KEY VERSE
v1

'Have mercy on me, O God, because of your unfailing love. Because of your great compassion, blot out the stain of my sins.'

NOBODY TALKS ABOUT sin any more. 'Sin' seems to be anachronistic – a concept that has no place in the twenty-first century world. I suppose that's because the word sounds judgmental and people don't like the idea that they should be answerable to someone for how they behave. Nobody wants to be told what to do or that how they're behaving is wrong in some way.

The trouble is our actions have consequences. Whether or not we like being told what to do, the way we behave has an impact on the world and the people around us. We can probably all think of occasions when our actions have hurt someone else, even on purpose. This, really, is what sin is. Sin means acting selfishly, ignoring how it will affect other people and what God might have to say about it all. That's something that has been true of all people, everywhere, throughout time and is likely to continue to be true forever. We're all guilty of ignoring God and hurting other people and for that reason we all need God's forgiveness.

PRAY

Ask God to forgive you for your sins. If you can think of anything specific you've done which hurt someone else, pray about that in particular. Receive God's forgiveness and pray that people you know will experience this forgiveness too.

WED 20 AUG

READ:
ISAIAH 64:1–7

KEY VERSE
v6

'We are all infected and impure with sin. When we display our righteous deeds, they are nothing but filthy rags.'

'BUT YOU DON'T need to be religious to be good.' Really? Well, what does 'good' mean? In order to be 'good', you need someone to decide what sort of behaviour is truly 'good' or 'evil' – someone to act as an ultimate moral authority. If we take God out of the equation, we're setting *ourselves* up as that authority. That is, we decide for ourselves what is good or evil and then behave in line with our own moral choices. Now, you don't need me to point out the obvious flaws with that idea. What if my view of what's 'good' is different to yours? Who's right? Who gets to decide whether another person's actions are truly good? Who has the right to say that? And what's to stop us from altering our own views of good and evil to justify doing something which, in our heart of hearts, we know is wrong?

In the end, it's impossible to live a 'good' life without acknowledging God as the authority on what 'good' means. He is the One who created us, who knows us better than we know ourselves and who is wise enough to know what is really best for us and for the whole human race.

CHALLENGE
Do you really live as if God is the One who decides what is truly 'good'? How would you explain why you do that, if someone asked?

READ: EPHESIANS 4:11–16

KEY VERSE
v15

'Instead, we will speak the truth in love, growing in every way more and more like Christ, who is the head of his body, the church.'

IMAGINE YOUR FRIEND spends £50 on a hair cut. They're delighted with their new style, but you think it's hideous. You can see it doesn't suit them at all, and people are starting to laugh at your friend behind their back. So what do you do? Surely you have to tell your friend the truth, so that they can get their hair sorted out. But if you're not careful what you say, you could really upset your friend and have a major falling-out. Telling the truth is important, but we need to choose our words with care.

While it's crucial that we're ready to stand up for what we believe in, we must be careful about how we do this. It's all too easy to get drawn into logical arguments with people who don't share our beliefs. But the more we argue, the less we communicate God's love to the person we're arguing with. Whatever we think of this person, God loves them. So let's not be afraid to share what we believe, but let's also remember to share our faith with *love*. Let's discuss and debate in a way that shows other people that God loves them – whether they believe in Him or not.

THINK

Who do you know who needs to hear about God? How can you share this with them while also showing them that God loves them?

FRI 22 AUG

READ:
MATTHEW 5:43–48

KEY VERSE
v44

'But I say, love your enemies! Pray for those who persecute you!'

WHO WOULD YOU call an enemy? Who makes your life hard? Perhaps the list of people you're thinking of includes some who keep telling you that your beliefs are childish and irrational and that faith in God is a waste of time. Whoever you consider an enemy, Jesus doesn't pull His punches here. He doesn't want us to merely tolerate our enemies; He wants us to love them! It won't be easy to love people who seem determined to undermine our faith and discredit our God, but this is what Jesus wants us to do. And by responding to their hostility with kindness, you're reflecting God's truth and goodness.

Maybe loving our enemies and praying for them go together. Perhaps it's as we pray for our enemies that God begins to show us how much He loves them. Maybe that process will begin to change us and will help us to love our enemies as God does. This won't mean accepting everything our enemies say, but it will mean being patient with them, keeping our temper under control and choosing to be a friend to them.

PRAY

Spend some time praying for your enemies – particularly people who try to undermine your faith. Pray for them by name, and ask Jesus to help you love each of these people, as He does.

1
2
3
4
5
6
7

READ:
ECCLESIASTES 3:9–13

KEY VERSE
V11

'He has planted eternity in the human heart ...'

CREATION PT3

IN OUR SERIES on 'Creation', we've already taken a look at the incredible world around us and what it can tell us about the God who made it. We've also thought about ourselves, and how God made us. We're now on our final lap on the 'Creation' series. To round it off, we'll think about God's plan for the people and the world He created. Why did God create us? How is God going to heal a suffering world? And how will all this end?

In today's reading, we find that an important part

7

CONTINUED»

CONTINUED»

of God's plan for each of us is to know Him. Inside us all there's a longing for something lasting, something meaningful and eternal. We're designed to have our needs met by God in order to be fulfilled. Some people describe this as being born with a 'God-shaped hole' inside us. People try to fill this hole with all sorts of things: work, alcohol, romance, drugs, even family. The problem is none of these really fill the hole: they'll all leave us unsatisfied.

There's nothing wrong with enjoying life and having a good time. In fact, all the good things that make life enjoyable are gifts from God. But in the end, the only thing that will really satisfy us is a relationship with God. Anything else will ultimately let us down and leave us lacking. God created us to know Him – and we're not truly living until we do.

CHALLENGE

Do you know God? Have you let Him take control of your life? If not, why not do so now? It's what you were created for.

If you already know God, spend some time this weekend talking to Him, listening to Him and getting to know Him better.

READ: EPHESIANS 2:8–10

KEY VERSE v10

'He has created us anew in Christ Jesus, so we can do the good things he planned for us long ago.'

WHEN I WAS at school, the last two or three weeks of the summer term were torture. We never did anything fun or productive. We just sat around, waiting for the holidays to start. I didn't want to be there, neither did my friends – and I suspect the teachers didn't either! The last days of term were spent gazing out of the window, staring at the clock (as if staring at it would make time pass faster) and praying for the holidays to come. When the final bell went on the final day of term, the sense of relief and freedom was huge. But, the funny thing is, within a week or two of being let out of school, I wanted to go back! Why? Because I was desperately bored. There was nothing to do. I had no sense of purpose.

There's nothing more guaranteed to make you bored, frustrated and depressed than the feeling of having no purpose. Fortunately we do have a purpose. God's plan for us is to do significant things that make a difference and which make earth more like heaven. God has created us to do good things. He's even planned out exactly what He wants each of us to do. God has an individual and unique purpose for each one of us. I don't know about you – but I feel good about that!

PRAY

Lord God, thank You that You've given me a unique purpose in life. Please help me to understand more clearly what that purpose is and exactly how You want me to live it out. Amen.

READ:
1 JOHN 3:1–3

KEY VERSE
v2

'But we do know that we will be like him, for we will see him as he really is.'

THINK BACK TO when you were five years old. What did you enjoy? What did you want to be when you grew up? How wise were you at that point? Maybe you were an exception, but not many people are wise or mature when they're five! It's as we grow up that we become wiser, more mature and, we might say, a more complete version of ourselves. When we look back at how we used to be, we often laugh at how little we really knew.

We've already mentioned several times that God created us to be like Him. We're His children. But we're not exactly like Him. Because we make mistakes, because we don't yet understand God completely, we're imperfect. But John assures us that one day, when we see Jesus face to face, we will be exactly like Him. As we follow God, we grow up, get wiser and start to show more godly qualities; and, in the end, we will be like Him, as we were always meant to be. One day we'll be perfect. One day we'll be like Jesus. That's our destiny. That's God's plan for us.

CHALLENGE

One day we will be like Jesus. But that doesn't mean we get out of trying to be like Him in the meantime! In fact we should try to keep ourselves pure. Take an honest look at your lifestyle. Is there anything there that needs to change so that you can be more pure and more like Jesus?

READ:
1 CORINTHIANS 2:7–10

WED 27 AUG

KEY VERSE
v9

'... no mind has imagined what God has prepared for those who love him.'

CAN YOU REMEMBER your first Christmas? Neither can I! However, my parents remember it very well. They tell me that I spent the days around Christmas with an expression of complete amazement all over my face. The presents, the cards, the decorations, the carols and the food were all completely new to me. Of course now I take all these things a bit for granted but, at the time, these were new, surprising, amazing things. I could never have imagined what Christmas would be like!

These verses from 1 Corinthians tell us that, in the same way, it's impossible to imagine the wonderful things God has planned for us. As we follow Jesus, we get a few glimpses of what He has in mind, but we've seen nowhere near all of it yet! God's plan for the people He created is not just to save them from their sin; it's to overwhelm them with wonderful and amazing things. We may not see those things this side of heaven, but one day we will.

PRAY

Thank God for His amazing plan and the wonderful things He has prepared for you.

THURS 28 AUG

READ:
MATTHEW 6:9-13

KEY VERSE
v10

'May your Kingdom come soon. May your will be done on earth, as it is in heaven.'

A FRIEND OF mine has just bought a house. It is a brand-new building, and he bought it before construction had even begun – it was just a patch of ground! Clearly this was a risk, but it meant that he could see his house taking shape, bit by bit. He saw the foundations being dug, the frame going up, the walls and roof being added, and the plumbing, electrics and carpets being arranged inside. The house started as a plan on a piece of paper and finished up as a physical building; the fulfilment of what the architect had planned. It was really exciting to see it all coming together!

God is an architect. He has a plan and He's building something wonderful. He's already created a world that's beautiful, but He has a plan to build on it and make it perfect. God's plan is to make earth like heaven. But the truly amazing thing is that God chooses to use us as His builders. God could just do it all Himself and make earth perfect before you could blink, but He chooses to work with us to make earth like heaven. God, the architect, has a plan and, if we act according to that plan, we help Him to build something incredible.

CHALLENGE

God wants us to work with Him to look after the planet. This means praying, but what else does it mean for you? Helping homeless people in your town? Campaigning against climate change? Or simply recycling more?

READ:
REVELATION 21:1–4

KEY VERSE
v3

'... God's home is now among his people! He will live with them ... they will be his people. God himself will be with them.'

YESTERDAY, WE THOUGHT about God's plan to make the earth perfect and the incredible privilege we have of playing a part in it. So, what happens when that part of God's plan is complete? These verses from Revelation answer that question. (Revelation is written in very symbolic language; we shouldn't get too hung up on why the sea has disappeared or why Jerusalem is coming down out of the sky.)

For us, the important focus is in verses 3–4. Once God's plan for the world He created is complete, He will come and be with us. Not just in the sense we know now – that He's with us through the Holy Spirit – but rather He will be powerfully and permanently present with us to comfort us and get rid of anything that's imperfect. In this new perfect world, death, pain and suffering will not exist. So if we're suffering now as a consequence of the imperfect world and people around us, we can be comforted by the knowledge that this won't last forever. But if we're tempted to just sit back and wait for God's plan to happen, we should remember that, in the meantime, we each have a unique part to play in that plan.

THINK

How does it make you feel to know that one day God will be with us and everything will be perfect? What can you do to play a part in God's plan in the meantime?

WEEKEND
30/31 AUG

READ:
REVELATION 21:5–7

KEY VERSE
v5
'Look, I am making everything new!'

WE BEGAN OUR studies on 'Creation' at the very beginning. We're ending at the very end. And God is still creating! At the very start of the Bible, God creates. At the very end, God recreates. He makes everything new, and everyone who follows Him will share in the blessings that this renewed, perfected world brings. God was the Creator in the beginning, He still is the Creator, and He always will be.

I like to keep myself as fit as I can. When I'm either injured or too busy to exercise, it's alarming how quickly I get out of shape. After just a couple of weeks of inactivity, my muscles turn to mush, my belly spreads and my heart and lungs feel like they've clogged up and gone to sleep. Keeping my body in shape is hard work. It's comforting to know that in the end God will renew my sluggish, creaking body and make it perfect.

While we're waiting for God's plan for creation to be fulfilled, and for this perfect world to happen, there are a few things we should remember. The world around us was created by God. He holds everything together, and everything in creation points us towards God and reminds us how great He is. Also, God's given us responsibility for looking after creation, and the chance to play a part in His plan to make it perfect. God made all the people around us too. He loves each of us, and wants us to know Him and let Him recreate us and give us new life.

Creation leaves us with a lot to think about!

THINK

What have you learned from our readings on 'Creation'? What do you want to say to God about it all? What has challenged you? What will you do differently from now on?

ORDER FORM

4 EASY WAYS TO ORDER:

1. For credit/debit card payment, call 01252 784710 (Mon–Fri, 9.30am – 5pm)
2. Visit our Online Store at www.cwr.org.uk/store
3. Send this form together with a cheque made payable to CWR to: CWR, Waverley Abbey House, Waverley Lane, Farnham, Surrey GU9 8EP
4. Visit a Christian bookshop

YOUR DETAILS	
Name:	
CWR ID No. (if known):	
Address:	
	Postcode:
Telephone No. (for queries):	
Email:	

SUBSCRIPTIONS (NON DIRECT DEBIT)	QTY	PRICE (INCLUDING P&P)			TOTAL
Mettle (1yr, 3 issues)*		**UK** £14.50	**Europe** £16.60	**Elsewhere** £18.75*	
(Subscription prices already include postage and packing)				**TOTAL** **B**	

Please circle which four-month issue you would like your subscription to commence from:

Jan–Apr **May–Aug** **Sep–Dec**

*Order direct from CWR or from your National Distributor. For a full list of our National Distributors and contact details, visit www.cwr.org.uk/distributors

eSubscription and eBooks available. Visit **www.cwr.org.uk/mettle** for details.